360° Feedback

Strategies, Tactics, and Techniques
for Developing Leaders

John E. Jones, Ph.D.
William L. Bearley, Ed.D.

ORGANIZATIONAL UNIVERSE SYSTEMS

HRD Press
&
Lakewood Publications

Copyright © 1996, Organizational Universe Systems

All rights reserved.

No part of this publication may be reproduced, transmitted, transcribed, stored in any type of retrieval system, or translated into any language in any form by any means without the prior written permission of the Publisher.

Organizational Universe Systems
P.O. Box 38
Valley Center, CA 92082
(619) 749-0811
(619) 749-8051 FAX

Published by: HRD Press   Lakewood Publications
               22 Amherst Road   50 South Ninth Street
               Amherst, MA 01002   Minneapolis, MN 55402
               (800) 466-4401   (800) 707-7769
               (413) 253-3490 FAX

ISBN # 0-87425-356-X

Cover Design by Marcelino Sellas
Editing by Mary George
Production Services by Susan Kotzin

TABLE OF CONTENTS

Chapter 1

Paradigm Shifts

Three major changes in organizational life have become clear during recent years, and each has implications for providing feedback to leaders. First, there has been an important shift in how we think about management and leadership. Second, people's careers within organizations have taken on new rules and responsibilities. And third, organizations have been expending considerable energy on improving their "cultures." These changes represent fundamental shifts in our views of how the organizational world works.

From Manager to Leader

Organizational leadership is undergoing a seismic shift. Senior executives are rapidly realizing that traditional notions of how to get work done through people just do not work well any longer. This requires, in a sense, turning the organization chart upside down and serving subordinates, or associates, rather than controlling them. Our discussion of the shift from emphasis on management to leadership, presented below, was developed in collaboration with Jeff McCollum, head of education and training at AT&T Consumer Products, and Dr. Richard O'Leary, manager of training at Owens Corning.

The change in emphasis compels leaders to operate from a different set of assumptions and to behave in ways that for some leaders differ from the norm; thus, ideally, leaders make significant changes in both their mental models and observable behavior. This shift also involves closing the gap between "the walk and the talk" on organizational values. Here are the chief changes that we believe are required.

- **From barriers to opportunities.** Managers tend strongly to focus on obstacles in the workplace. They are socialized to fix things, to remove barriers. Leaders need to consider the possibilities, rather than the problems, in a business situation.

- **From control of staff to processes that yield results.** The scorecard in many business and industrial organizations stresses the manager's span of control. Leaders need to think in terms of process, as is emphasized in all total-quality efforts.

- **From competition to collaboration.** Perhaps the most distinctive part of managerial programming shows up at work as interpersonal competition. Managers often seem preoccupied with winning, and working in highly competitive organizations adds stress to the work itself. If the organization is in competitive markets, the situation is often exacerbated; managers take an inflexible, win-lose stance in relation to other "players" in the market-place, and they exhibit competitive behavior even towards their peers inside organizational groups.

- **From compliance to commitment.** Managers tend to want to lead rather than to be led, to control rather than to conform, to leave room for exit. Since organizations no longer offer employees long-term security, employees must turn to managing their employability, and they show commitment "so long as it is working for me."

- **From controlling to coaching.** Unconsciously managers show a need to be in charge at all times. They attempt to impose boundaries more often than focus on developing their people. Coaching is softer; it requires sensitivity and patience. For the most part, managers are rewarded for financial results, not for developing their people.

- **From directing to participating.** There has been considerable emphasis in recent years on participative management, empowerment, and employee involvement. In our consulting on these subjects with managers, the essential issue is *always* fear of loss of control. Managers need to learn the counter-intuitive notion that giving their power away actually increases it.

- **From either/or, linear thinking to generative, inclusive thinking.** Managers tend to think categorically and linearly, rather than laterally and creatively. They need to move from black-and-white models to shades of gray, with loose categories, if any.

- **From exclusionary to inclusionary.** Communication networks in organizations are often notoriously exclusionary. Managers need to examine their personal values in this regard and move toward inviting and soliciting the active participation of employees whom they see as different from themselves. Valuing diversity may mean a large shift in personal orientation on the part of some managers. This shift offers the promise of improved results. The WIIFM Factor ("What's In It For Me?") permeates organizations. Managers tend to reinforce it by focusing on individual contributors rather than team players. Leaders need to shift the discussion to such orientations as, "None of us is as smart as all of us," and "Unless we hang together, we'll all hang separately."

- **From extrinsic rewards to intrinsic motivations.** Managers often use the carrot-and-stick approach to motivation. They make little or no attempt to find out what motivates others. Managers need to focus on self-directed behavior, on providing inspiration and links to how people can get what they want from the work.

- **From premature problem solving to consultation.** Many managers search for a quick fix as an automatic response to business and industrial situations that need attention. This can be a means by which others come to depend on them, and it can give them a chance to be heroes. The developmental need, however, is to learn how to provide consultative assistance in ways that help others learn.

- **From holding information and power to sharing knowledge and power.** In our experience, most managers view power as a fixed quantity. They do not understand that the fundamental paradox is that sharing it increases it. Women seem far more open to facilitating the empowerment of others. Leaders become empowered by their followers. They understand the adage "Unless there are followers, there are no leaders."

- **From internal standards to customer specifications.** The radical idea that drives total quality management—that quality is not inherent in things but exists only in the perceptions of customers—requires that managers rethink their work in terms of *relationships* rather than *things*. Leaders build long-term, mutually satisfying relationships.

- **From managing behavior to generating results.** Performance management, although it can appear to resemble micro-teaching, is often experienced by employees as micro-management. Managers need to move from a controlling, checking stance to a posture that emphasizes getting outcomes that are prized by both the organization and its people. Leaders invoke the power of vision to get results through people.

- **From motivation to self-responsibility.** Managers still ask us in training courses, "How do I motivate my people?" It is as though managers think that they need to put something into others in order to move them. The leadership view begins with the presupposition that people *are* motivated. The idea is to help them see links between what the organization wants and what's in it for them.

- **From perfection to customer expectations.** While baseball players can earn over a million dollars each year while batting .250 (failing three out of four times at bat), many managers strive for perfection. Leaders need rather to approach tasks not in terms of absolutes but in terms of what customers need, want, and expect.

- **From power plays to persuasion.** Managers overrely on power to get what they want. This approach does not work in sales, of course, but managers still tend to "pull rank" and use other power tactics to win. The need here is to transcend this socialization and to learn how to act persuasively but not necessarily argumentatively.

- **From projects, tasks, and responsibilities to meeting customer needs.** Managers tend to show a decided bias toward being task-oriented rather than people-oriented. The need here is to expand one's viewpoint, to see the interrelatedness of social and technical aspects of work. The coalescing factor is meeting customer specifications, and that process is inextricably interpersonal as well as technical.

- **From quality control to continuous improvement.** An extension of the male need for control is having an orientation toward quality that is exemplified by the traditional emphasis on quality control. Synergistic thinking about quality focuses on how products and services are perceived by customers, and technical analyses center on making incremental improvements in organization-specific work processes and in how customers get satisfied.

- **From clear roles and rules to whatever it takes to serve customers.** Managers see this shift as moving from a clear set of rules to an uncertain game. Managers tend to want to nail down everything. They are uncomfortable with ambiguity, and they construct organizations and work processes that can become bureaucratic, slow, and expensive. Modern organizations require that managers learn how to organize people and work tasks in highly flexible ways, so that changes in the marketplace can be anticipated and even led profitably. Managers invented job descriptions, and they perpetuate this kind of structural form in the extreme by expressing the counterproductive attitude, "That's not my job." Managers need to adopt the idea of customer focus rather than make decisions solely on the basis of their role in the order of things.

- **From spending or downsizing to investing.** Since budget size seems to be psychologically correlated with the male ego ("Mine's bigger than yours"), managers tend to work from the premise "If I don't spend it, I won't get it next year." Alternatively, they tend to "slash and burn" in order to reduce costs when the desired financial results are not present. Rewarding these behaviors has cost organizations dearly. There is a need for managers to think more in terms of developing people and systems to produce a return on investment, and less in terms of managing a budget.

- **From structure to facilitation.** Organizational structures can be thought of as ways of controlling people's behavior in the absence of management. Policies, rules, official procedures, regulations, rewards, systems, organizational charts—all these aspects of structure become reified, and they can seriously jeopardize the ability of organizations to meet the changing priorities of customers in the global marketplace. Managers need to think more along the lines of making things easy, and less of worst-case scenarios and organizing to prevent difficulties. Empowerment means, among other things, stripping away impediments to the full participation of employees, and the facilitative leader emphasizes developing the ability of people to flourish within the goals of the organization.

Thinking as leaders rather than as managers means behaving in ways that are consistent with the assumptions underlying the changes in the above list. This means learning how to see subordinates as the people who do the work and leaders as facilitators of that process. Leaders then act to create an environment that brings out the best in subordinates, with the fewest impediments to their personal growth, creativity, and productivity. Here is what this new paradigm of work requires of leaders.

Show a passion for the work. Some people tend to think that it is not OK to show emotion at work. It is not only OK to show emotion about work, it is imperative that each leader be genuinely "turned-on" by what subordinates are doing. Expressing enthusiasm leads to the attitude "I can make a substantial difference here."

Enroll people in vision. Bennis and Nanus (1985, p. 19) promote "leading others, managing yourself." How leaders do this is by developing a vision of a desirable and doable future for the organization and working with its people to see the connections between what the organization is doing and their reasons for working here.

Take risks, make mistakes, test limits. Playing it safe does not move the organization forward. Letting go of power may increase it. Delegating may free the leader from routine and enrich the work of subordinates. Challenging outdated processes, procedures, regulations, and norms may lead to beneficial change.

Look for opportunities. In competitive environments it is up to each leader actively to seek methods of improving the organization in every way possible. This means paying attention to the details of how work gets done, searching for soft spots in work processes. Time and space, once regarded as constraints, can be a marketing edge. Products and services that meet customers "any time and any place" will win in the company's market.

Involve people in decisions that affect them. Leaders need commitment, not agreement or conformity. That means that people have to feel influential with regard to what gets done and how. Leaders need to facilitate participation in decision making, problem solving, action planning, and change efforts in ways that result in people being willing to invest *themselves* in their work.

Eat problems for lunch. Leaders need to consider the situations that arise in work areas as opportunities for improvement rather than as headaches or distractions. Problems can be their best teachers if leaders are open to working with the problems rather than simply trying to "solve" them. In addition, leaders need to communicate this positive attitude to subordinates.

Eliminate "either/or thinking." Leaders cannot let themselves think of an action as either being for the company's owners or being for its people. Leaders need action that serves both. Neither can they let themselves think in terms of having either high quality or low cost. Leaders need action that accomplishes both.

Assure that words and actions are congruent. Subordinates will infer what leaders expect of them by focusing on the actions of leaders. When their actions and words are not aligned, their words will be ignored. The shared values of the organization are not concepts—they are a way of life. Leaders have a special responsibility to align their behavior with these values and to help subordinates learn how to do the same. Leaders are, in a sense, behavioral manifestations of these values.

Hold self and others accountable. There should be no place to hide in the organization. Each leader and his or her people are paid to contribute to the long-term financial viability of the organization. This means appraising the performance of subordinates honestly and skillfully. It also means confronting people who do not live up to their agreements.

Become obsessed with customer needs. Each work group has both suppliers and customers for the products and services of the organization. Leaders need to move toward a condition of partnership with these people. This means thinking in customer-supplier terms all of the time.

Negotiate nonmanipulatively. The one thing that leaders can count on is change, and this requires renegotiation of expectations of each other. It also means adjusting expectations of subordinates' responsibilities and procedures. In the process of leading people, they need to make these changes in win-win ways.

Maximize quality while minimizing costs. Using quality technology can help the organization to continuously improve how work gets done. This is a great deal of the "how" of leadership. "Big Q" quality means acting as leaders to infuse a mentality that prevents rework and strives to satisfy all customers and partners all of the time.

Focus on ROI. Profitability serves the organization's people, owners, and customers. If the organization remains profitable, its leaders provide people with prospects of continued employment and advancement. If the company is profitable, its leaders are effective stewards of the company owners' investment. If the organization is profitable, its people serve customers by staying in business to meet their needs now and in the future.

Making the shift from manager to leader means looking honestly at behavior vis-à-vis other people and moving toward a developmental (rather than a control) posture. Many organizational leaders say, "Our people are our greatest asset." It is time for each leader to live out the implications of that belief each day. All of this argues for the institutionalization of a new set of behavioral norms. What is needed is a commitment to a new paradigm of work.

The Big Shift in Career Development

The changes that have evolved during recent years regarding career development within organizations have been dramatic and unnerving to many. There has been a fundamental shift in the rules of the game, in responsibilities, practices, and programs. Employees, including leaders, can no longer count on the organization to take care of their careers for them. Now it is the individual's responsibility. The "womb-to-tomb" norm has changed irrevocably. The employee must take a proactive stance, managing his or her career as a personal project, using the resources and support available within the organization. This paradigm shift has caused consternation on the part of many workers, especially middle managers who had been counting on upward mobility and instead became an endangered species as organizations flattened their hierarchies. These days it is not uncommon to see responsibility as a clearly stated organizational value.

This new emphasis on self-direction in career planning requires that the organization provide solid information to the individual for the purpose of personal and professional development. Since the performance-review process rarely gives the individual the proper information on which to base career plans, an alternative source of information is needed. The process of 360° assessment fulfills this need, providing the individual with a more holistic, useful set of data that can greatly facilitate career planning.

Focus on Organizational Culture

In recent years, both large and small organizations have spent considerable time, energy, and funds on elucidating and propagandizing their mission, purposes, visions, and values. The whole of this activity has been in the service of organizational "culture change." Anthropologists argue over the meaning of culture, but organizational leaders operationally define it in terms of statements.

One wag said, "Culture is what people do and monkeys don't." The emphasis on aligned behavior has followed the issuance of corporate statements. What is needed is for everyone in the organization to have a common understanding of the organization's reason for existence, its future direction, and what it stands for. Then it is the leaders' responsibility to ensure that all employees act in ways that are consistent with the organization's stated values, that they actively support the realization of its vision, and that they clearly understand how their work contributes to carrying out the organization's mission.

What Necessitates 360° Feedback

These three paradigm shifts—from manager to leader, from dependency to self-responsibility in career planning, and from traditional hierarchy to culture-focused organizational change—require that the organization give its employees the information they need to guide their own development. As mentioned earlier, this requirement can be successfully met through the use of 360° feedback. Leaders need such feedback to inform them of their strengths and weaknesses in ways that generate confidence in the numbers. Individual contributors and team members need 360° feedback to plan career-enhancing moves. The organization needs the results of this feedback to monitor trends in its human resources, with this tracking clearly linked to what is required to actualize the organization's vision.

Basically, the term 360° feedback refers to the practice of gathering and processing multirater assessments on individuals and feeding back the results to these participants. Typically the process involves ratings by self, boss, peers, and subordinates; the feedback reports are usually confidential. What 360° feedback does is help leaders solve what we have termed the IDKWIS problem. The acronym refers to the situation in which leaders are in the dark regarding their position within the organization. The IDKWIS problem statement reads like a chemical formula:

$$NETMA + NEAMO + INA = IDKWIS$$

NETMA	Nobody ever tells me anything.
+	
NEAMO	Nobody ever asks my opinion.
+	
INA	I never ask.
=	
IDKWIS	I don't know where I stand.

Leaders obviously need to know where they stand, especially during the changes that have been alluded to in this chapter. As we experience the shift in our fundamental view of how organizational worlds work, we more critically need to know how we are being perceived (and judged) by significant others in our work situations. Providing 360° feedback enables leaders to shift their thinking about themselves and about getting work done through others during a time in which organizational life is becoming increasingly complex. Knowing where you stand at any given moment is vital information for determining how you fit into the model that the organization is espousing; it facilitates developing collaborative relationships with both colleagues and team members, and it provides a basis for career-development planning.

Organizations are rapidly adopting 360° feedback. Timmreck (1995) cites a survey of a corporate consortium, formed in 1993, whose 20 large companies routinely utilize upward feedback or 360° assessments. Survey results indicated that over half use the methods company-wide. The data are used for development and coaching in 93% of the companies, with 28% utilizing it as input for appraisal. A majority (56%) of these organizations conduct such assessments annually, using printed forms. Over half (55%) use all direct reports as raters, and 59% also collect self-ratings. Very few (3%) of these organizations use off-the-shelf instruments. On average, there are 45 items in their questionnaires. Over three-quarters of the companies use outside vendors to process the data and prepare the feedback reports.

The use of 360° feedback offers many benefits both to feedback recipients and to their organizations. Hoffman (1995) calls our attention to 10 of these benefits, pointing out that such feedback does the following:

1. Defines corporate competencies

2. Increases the focus on customer service

3. Supports team initiatives

4. Creates a high-involvement work force

5. Decreases hierarchies and promotes streamlining

6. Detects barriers to success

7. Assesses developmental needs

8. Avoids discrimination and bias

9. Identifies performance thresholds

10. Is easy to implement

Carey (1995) predicted that about 30% of companies will use the technology by the year 2000. Bracken (1994, p. 49) points out that organizations are embracing multirater feedback for five major reasons:

1. Such systems complement other initiatives, such as empowerment and participative management, the removal of management layers, and the emphasis on teamwork

2. Multirater feedback overcomes some of the limitations of traditional appraisal methods in organizations where supervisors have wider spans of control.

3. Other methods, such as employee surveys, have not generated increases in accountability and follow-through on the part of managers.

4. Customized 360° feedback instruments can become concrete statements of what competencies are needed to actualize the senior leaders' vision.

5. Multirater assessment is intuitively more believable because the pooling of data collected from different perspectives could provide more accuracy.

Shaver (1995, p. 13) points out that 360° assessment helps people uncover expectations, strengths, and weaknesses that are news to them; it broadens the perspective on evaluating an individual by using multiple data sources; it provides ratings that can become benchmarks in the feedback recipient's performance-appraisal process; it may promote people becoming increasingly accountable for their own growth and development; and it is an efficient procedure in that it is inexpensive, simple, and quick

Clearly, 360° feedback is catching on. Although it initially makes some participants feel apprehensive, it has been found to add value to the career and personal-development planning of a growing number of personnel who are eager to find out where they stand in the organization.

About This Book

We conducted a survey of the users of our software systems in order to determine the emphases needed in this book. Professionals who routinely use 360° assessment and feedback told us that a practical manual was needed—a "how-to" book that lays out steps to take and traps to avoid. They also indicated that they were using this technology in a wide array of applications inside their client organizations. The methods described in this book reflect the flexibility of applying 360° assessment and feedback for various purposes

The chapters have been arranged with the reader's convenience in mind, to make it easy to use the book as a handy reference. In this chapter we have discussed why the technology is important for moving organizations toward a leadership posture, for helping employees manage their own careers, and for facilitating the movement toward modern organizational cultures. The next chapter explains in detail what 360° assessment and feedback is and how it generally works. Chapters 3 to 9 illustrate specific applications of this technology for different purposes inside organizations. Chapters 10 to 17 provide detailed methods for optimizing the use of 360° assessment and feedback. Chapter 18 focuses on the technical considerations of reliability and validity as they relate to this type of assessment, and the final chapter gives concrete suggestions on how to get started in using these methods

The appendices to this book can be invaluable references for the user. Appendix A includes a reproducible worksheet to facilitate the planning of applications of 360° assessment and feedback. In Appendix B we include worksheets for action planning. Appendix C contains a generic instrument that you can use in developing your organization's competency model. In Appendix D we present a worksheet that generates differential weights for various data sources, or types of raters, in case the organization wants to attach different credibility to each.

A note about terminology. In this book we refer to the recipients of 360° assessment and feedback as "leaders." That is because in most uses of this technology the targets are organizational executives, managers, and supervisors. We believe strongly that they should be undergoing the shift that is described in this chapter, from management to leadership. It is important to point out that the methodology of 360° assessment and feedback can be used with anyone, whether in a formal position of leadership or not. In a sense, the modern organization, with its emphasis on self-management, is not so much "leaderless" as "leader*ful*." Everyone influences everyone else in a dynamic mix of interpersonal relationships that serve the organization's mission and vision and meet the needs of its people simultaneously. In this book we refer to providing feedback to leaders; read this as referring to any or all employees.

Chapter 2

Assessment and Feedback

It is important to make a sharp distinction between leadership and management, as we discussed in Chapter 1. In addition, it is important to distinguish between assessment and feedback. *Assessment is measurement, not evaluation.* Assessment may take the form of interviews, questionnaires, surveys, or observations. *Feedback is information that tells a leader how others in the organization perceive the leader and/or how the leader's behavior is affecting the organization.* Feedback may take the form of statistical data, verbal confrontations, financial reports, or appraisal interviews. The distinction is important because when we develop interventions that include 360° feedback, we need to be careful to separate the data gathering from the analysis of the results. The proper locus of evaluation in 360° feedback is the recipient of the feedback, not the persons who provide their perceptions through questionnaires.

Effective and Destructive Feedback

To equip leaders with effective feedback, we must ensure that our feedback meets 14 basic criteria. Feedback that successfully meets these criteria can be described as:

1. **Individualized** (Daniels, 1989, p. 186).
2. **Clear and unambiguous.** Feedback should be open to only one interpretation.
3. **Accurately worded.** We should check feedback to assure that what a recipient hears is what was intended.
4. **Well presented.** In presenting feedback, we should give recipients the opportunity to ask for clarification of anything they do not understand about the feedback.

5. **Focused on modifiable behavior.** A recipient cannot improve behavior if the behavior is impossible to change.

6. **Goal-directed.** The information contained in the feedback should focus on goals, and the goals should be "bought into" by the recipient.

7. **Timely.** The feedback should center on the recent or current behavior of the recipient.

8. **Affirming and reinforcing.** The feedback should bring to light, and bolster, the recipient's strengths.

9. **Sensitive.** We should provide feedback that is sensitive to the recipient's needs and receptivity.

10. **Unforced.** People are more receptive to feedback that is solicited rather than imposed.

11. **Descriptive.** Descriptive feedback is preferable to evaluative information: "Here's how you appear" is almost always more useful than "Here's how I judge you."

12. **Specific.** Specific information is clearly more useful than general information: "When you interrupt me while I am speaking, I tend to become frustrated and angry" is more useful than "You're a dominant person."

13. **Validated.** Feedback needs validation, that is, it must be checked with others in the organization to determine how extensively the feedback giver's perceptions are shared by others.

14. **Charted.** The recipient should chart the feedback on a graph (Daniels, 1989, p. 190).

Feedback is powerful information and a potent experience. It can build or break down relationships, and it can mislead as well as inform. Here are some characteristic elements of destructive feedback:

1. **Evaluation and judgment.** For example, "Your output may rate 4 on a 5-point scale, but you had better get your act together when it comes to getting along with people."

2. **Insensitivity to the recipient's ability to use the feedback productively.** An example would be giving too much feedback on results while a person is still learning a new task.

3. **Distortion of the recipient's self-understanding.** Such feedback leaves the recipient in a state of self-doubt: "I thought I knew myself well, but now I'm not so sure."
4. **Poor timing.** For instance, telling the recipient "You really alienated me by what you did three years ago."
5. **Labeling.** "You're clearly a Driver Driver" is an example. This is a type of hard-driving profile used in social-styles instruments.
6. **Discounting ("writing the person off as a bad debt").** Constructive feedback is withheld because of doubts about the recipient's ability to change.
7. **Indirect delivery of feedback.** For example, telling a third party about problems with a co-worker rather than confronting the co-worker.
8. **Innuendo.** Feedback via innuendo is often derogatory: "I don't know what your agenda is, but I'm sure the team will want to go forward in spite of it."
9. **Faint praise.** "She's pretty good—about a 4, I'd say" is an example.
10. **A focus on the recipient's intentions.** Such feedback is more concerned about what the recipient is "up to" than what the recipient can do to improve his or her organizational position.

Providing specific yet descriptive, nonjudgmental feedback to leaders in a sensitive and timely manner is not an easy task. One deterrent to the process is the strong tendency of organizational members to withhold information—to collude not to "tell it like it is." Senior author John E. Jones (Pfeiffer & Jones, 1972) co-developed a model of the situation, which is shown below.

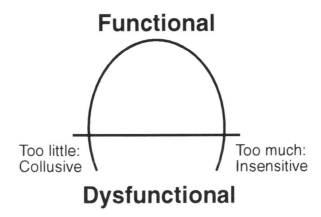

Functional

Too little:
Collusive

Too much:
Insensitive

Dysfunctional

The model represents a continuum in the shape of a horseshoe, indicating that too much openness is just as dysfunctional as too little (collusion). In other words, too much of a good thing may not be good; the optimum situation is not linear. To help us determine how openly we should provide feedback in any given situation, Pfeiffer and Jones (1972) offer a simple method based on the concept of "strategic openness." This method involves sensing the comfort level of the feedback recipient, then going 10 to 15 percent beyond that level. Through the strategy of pushing beyond the recipient's comfort level, we are able to open up the relationship to a productive degree as well as avoid collusion.

"Informing" leaders through 360° feedback also means "in-forming" them: clarifying expectations, identifying strengths, and pointing out opportunities for improvement. The development process begins with the solicitation of data, then proceeds to the data's interpretation and toward a commitment for implementation of a self-directed action plan. The plan should lead to the leader acting out his or her strategy, measuring results, and soliciting further feedback.

Much of the information that is fed back to leaders is more subjective than objective. Using questionnaires and rating scales simply standardizes the stimuli for describing or judging the feedback recipient and recording the results. It is not necessary to engage in a lengthy consideration of the nature of reality in order to make sense out of 360° feedback. An old saying goes, "Whatever appears to be is *always* more important than what is." The definition of reality underpinning 360° feedback is essentially phenomenological: people's perceptions drive their job performance and their evaluation of others' performance and competencies. Learning what those perceptions are can be invaluable for "correcting" one's view of self and for making choices in the workplace. Unfortunately, feelings and judgments can complicate the act of providing useful feedback to leaders.

It is important to remember three points:

- Good feedback is simply information. It is not an assessment of the individual's worth as a leader or as a person.
- Interpersonal feedback is inherently subjective.
- In the leader-development process, the proper locus of evaluation is the individual who receives the information.

Why Soliciting Feedback Is Important

There are five major reasons why it is important for leaders to ask for feedback on their traits, competencies, and behavioral practices.

1. It provides answers to the vital self-management question, "How am I doing?" As leaders rise in the hierarchy they receive less and less honest information about themselves, and 360° assessment and feedback can provide them with the information they need to take corrective action.

2. Asking for feedback can be a guidance mechanism for continuous improvement. If the total quality movement leaves a legacy to future organizations, it will probably be the notion of steadily making efforts to improve everything that bears on the mission of the organization. For leaders to apply that notion to themselves, and serve as models for others, they must have reliable, valid, timely information on how they are perceived.

3. The use of 360° assessment and feedback can help leaders validate their self-perceptions. Most leaders do not obtain their positions through random behavior, and they know it. They do, however, need honest feedback from others to test their own understanding of their strengths and weaknesses.

4. It has been observed that people are the only animals capable of self-deception. We need feedback from trusted others in order to ensure that we are viewing ourselves realistically.

5. Perhaps most important, 360° assessment and feedback gets people to invest in the effectiveness of leaders. Soliciting feedback from bosses, peers, subordinates, customers, and others actively involves them in a process of improvement, and they are more likely to support leaders who ask for feedback, act on it, and follow through with them afterwards.

Soliciting feedback is consistent with the modern emphasis on self-management in organizations.

Common Practices

The practice of providing 360° feedback is not new. Numerous organizations have been engaged in developing their managers and leaders through this method. In later chapters of this book, we will explore several common uses of 360° feedback. Here are the most frequent uses:

- Using 360° feedback as a system intervention
- Using it as a component of team building
- Incorporating 360° feedback into courses
- Assessing training needs with 360° surveys
- Embedding upward feedback into employee surveys
- Assessing outcomes of training
- Return-on-investment analyses regarding leadership-development schemes
- Linking 360° feedback and performance appraisal

The 360° feedback technology is robust, and its many applications attest to its appeal as a mechanism for letting leaders know where they stand.

How the 360° Assessment and Feedback Process Usually Works

This methodology usually is implemented through a linear set of steps, as follows:

1. **Determine the need for, and purpose(s) of, the assessment.** This entails setting up objectives for the use of 360° assessment and feedback. Validity is directly connected to purpose in such instrumentation, and no instrument should be expected to be valid for all the uses to which this technology is put.

2. **Establish a competency model.** If the assessment focuses on competencies, it is best to work from some sort of model that shows how the competency elements are linked to one another and/or to meaningful criteria of success (see Chapter 10).

3. **Weight data sources and select and develop assessment items.** Since 360° assessment involves gathering ratings from several people about one person, it is important to consider the data source and determine whether data from separate sets of raters will be treated equally or weighted differently (see Appendix D). Sometimes organizations want to study their leadership cadres according to some sort of weighted average of their 360° feedback ratings. We recommend that this practice be rarely employed, unless there is some

compelling need to generate weighted data. It can greatly complicate the feedback process. Developing items means adapting them to a rating format and wording them in clear language that everyone understands the same way (see Chapter 14).

4. **Develop an assessment questionnaire.** After determining the items that will be used in the 360° assessment instrument, the next step is to develop the actual questionnaire. Instructions for the questionnaire should emphasize the importance of the survey and assure raters that their anonymity will be protected. Other considerations (discussed in Chapter 14) include the choice of a rating scale, the format for responding to the items, and the overall look and feel of the instrument. Also, it can be helpful to construct two forms of the questionnaire: a self-assessment form, which will be completed by the feedback recipients, and an "other" form, which will be completed by the feedback givers (see next step).

5. **Administer the questionnaire.** The easiest way of gathering 360° feedback data is to collect self-assessments in meetings in which you also distribute "other"-rating questionnaires to the participants, who then give them to the people from whom they want to solicit feedback. Whatever method is used, it is vital to caution participants who will receive the feedback not to attempt to bias the responses of their feedback sources and to assure these "others" that their data will be treated anonymously. Bosses' ratings, of course, are not anonymous, but they should be kept confidential, shown only to the feedback recipient. Since 360° feedback can seem threatening to some individuals, it may be advantageous to use an outside agency to receive and process the questionnaires.

6. **Process the data and develop feedback reports.** The primary concerns in this step are speed, accuracy, safety, and security. Consider using answer sheets and scanning equipment for data entry, to minimize human error. Carefully consider the form of feedback reports, since the focus is on understanding and development, not on statistical complexity (see Chapter 15).

7. **Deliver the feedback reports ("cascade").** In a 360° feedback system intervention, reports are usually delivered in a series of meetings, or sessions, with each meeting devoted to a different leadership level. The design of these meetings emphasizes three things: confidentiality, the development of an understanding of the statistical results, and the facilitation of personal, self-directed action planning for improvements, including following through with

one's raters, enrolling them in supporting the plan (see Chapter 16). The meetings begin at the top of the organization and work down through the "ranks," so that any given leader's manager will experience the process before the leader does.

8. **Brief the executive on group trends.** After all of the feedback reports have been worked through by individual leaders at all levels of the organization, the human resource staff studies the overall data set. The broad findings equip the senior leaders to consider the development of their leadership cadre as a strategic organizational objective.

9. **Evaluate the intervention.** The design of an evaluation of the 360° feedback system intervention should be approved by the executive group. This may include a reassessment after a year and the development of employee-attitude-survey items that can track progress in the improvement of leadership.

Variations on these steps will be described in the following chapters.

The Major Benefits of 360° Assessment and Feedback

Providing 360° assessment and feedback information to leaders about how they are perceived by significant others in their work environment can have enormous benefits, both to the individual and to the organization (O'Reilly, 1994). Here are the major benefits:

1. The assessment is systematic—structured so that it can be repeated and validated.

2. The process sharply targets the self-directed improvement plans of the individual leaders.

3. Thoroughly working through the data before proceeding to the self-directed action plans can lay the groundwork for a genuine commitment to following through on the plans.

4. 360° assessment and feedback can be accurately aligned with the overall development thrusts of the organization (the contents of the questionnaire can send a clear message to leaders: "Here is what you need to become good at in order to help us realize our organizational vision").

5. 360° assessment and feedback can form the basis for a tracking system to determine the results and payoffs of developmental programs in organizational leadership; repeat studies on groups of leaders should show improvement over time if the organization's training and development efforts are effective.

These payoffs derive mostly from the personal nature of the process—its emphasis on providing solid information to the individual for action planning.

Chapter 3

360° Feedback as a
System Intervention

The most powerful use of 360° feedback in organizations is as a pervasive intervention, a method that involves all supervisory personnel and, in some cases, subordinate personnel. This chapter briefly describes the strategies and techniques commonly used in such interventions. Usually the objective relates to the realization of a new vision for the future of the organization—a vision that may call for a shift toward the paradigms outlined in Chapter 1.

Case Examples

At one large telecommunications company, the senior-management team drove a process that provided 360° feedback to approximately 3000 managers over a year's time. A survey of 200 randomly selected managers revealed the needed competencies for the actualization of the goals of the business, and the senior executives independently rated these skills. Over three days the team worked with the list of competencies and produced a questionnaire. Data were gathered from the managers themselves and their bosses, peers, and subordinates ("associates"). The manner of data collection was unique in that raters called a toll-free number and coded in their responses (see Chapter 5 for additional information on this technique). Feedback was a key part of a week-long training program, Project Leadership, which senior author John E. Jones designed. Norms for the instrument were accumulated weekly, making the feedback increasingly rich in focus. Over 36,000 sets of ratings were collected. The Education Division and senior-executive team also benefited from statistical summaries of trends by management level and location.

A leading brewing company wanted to implement the Skills Management System for its marketing and sales personnel. Eleven highly specific 360° feedback instruments covered the key jobs, and incumbents solicited feedback from their bosses, peers (when appropriate), and customers (non-anonymous, by the way, so that sales representatives could contact them afterwards to close any identified perception gaps). Company facilitators delivered the feedback in half-day sessions in the field, with people from various jobs present. The policy was for each individual to achieve consensus on one set of ratings with his or her supervisor—within 24 hours—and to get the supervisor's "sign off" on an action plan for development. The final numbers were then keyed into the Skills Management System software for tracking improvements. Company organization-development personnel benefitted from the training-needs assessment that automatically resulted from the process. The skills that came up as opportunities for improvement across these jobs were targeted for additional training and development initiatives.

At a second telecommunications company, advertising representatives for the Yellow Pages benefited from 360° feedback by soliciting data from their bosses, peers, and selected customers. An instrument was developed by a task force and then administered by mail throughout 14 states. Field salespeople received feedback in regional meetings and enrolled their division managers in supporting their self-directed action plans. These people were so enthusiastic about the experience that the senior managers decided to repeat the process for all supervisors in field marketing and sales, and the task force was assigned to adapt the survey instrument for this use. Again, feedback was delivered in regional meetings; the worksheets in Appendix B formed the basis of the action-planning sessions.

At a health maintenance organization, senior executives embarked on a major effort to improve quality of service. A 360° feedback intervention for doctors who manage doctors set a precedent for looking at skills and behavior as they relate to customer satisfaction with medical services. The survey instrument focused on management and supervisory skills. At another health-maintenance-organization facility, a system was established in which randomly selected customers rated doctors immediately after receiving treatment. Doctors then compared these ratings with their self-assessments and those of their supervisors.

The Cascade Strategy

System interventions such as the ones described above involve large numbers of people, sometimes including people outside the organization. It is therefore essential to think through the steps of such interventions in advance and to be well prepared to take those steps. The most ideal approach to using 360° feedback as a system intervention, presented below, is faithful to the nine-step process methodology that was discussed in Chapter 2. Whereas some steps are virtually identical to their numeric counterparts in the basic process method, others have been modified to fit the unique needs of system intervention. Also, keep in mind that this is an *ideal* approach and, consequently, must be adapted to an organization's particular needs and conditions. The important point is twofold: that steps similar to the following are necessary, and that they must be specified before the intervention begins.

1. **Obtain executive buy-in.** A good method is to conduct a senior-leadership intervention by providing 360° feedback to members of the executive team, so that they can discover its usefulness. The instrument for such a study should correlate closely with the stated purpose and vision of the organization. A related way to get buy-in is to solicit the executive's final approval of the content and process of any leadership-feedback instrument that will be used with their subordinates. When 360° feedback becomes a component of a management-development training course, such as the one referred to above in the first case example, it is important that senior executives accept the responsibility to act as model participants, using their results with their people in ways that make the process credible and less threatening than it can be.

2. **Conduct a survey on needed competencies.** As illustrated by the first case example, it is important to isolate those skills and competencies that are necessary to carry out the mission and realize the vision of the organization. A survey of representative personnel can reveal what it will take to be successful in the future organization. A stratified random sample of supervisory personnel, department managers, and others below the level of senior management can provide the basis for determining needed competencies. Data also can be collected in meetings and "grab groups," but the results may be misleading. The survey of needed competencies should be comprehensive, should center on the vision/mission/purpose of the organization, and should be endorsed by the executive team.

3. **Weight data sources and select competency items.** As mentioned in Chapter 2, since 360° feedback involves gathering ratings from several people about one person, it is important to consider the data source and determine whether data from separate sets of raters will be treated equally or weighted differentially. Appendix D contains a worksheet that helps establish different weights for different data sources. The worksheet is best used in an off-site session with senior managers, where they not only carry out this task but also select the final items for the survey instrument, draft new items, and go through the "wordsmithing" that is sometimes required for buy-in.

4. **Develop an assessment questionnaire.** After determining the competency items, the next step is to develop the actual questionnaire. Often, self-rating and "other"-rating forms are constructed. Instructions for the questionnaire should emphasize the importance of the survey and guarantee the raters' anonymity. Other considerations include the choice of a rating scale, the format for responding to the items, and the overall look and feel of the instrument.

5. **Administer the questionnaire.** The easiest way of gathering 360° feedback data is, as noted earlier, to collect self-assessments in meetings in which you also distribute "other"-rating questionnaires to the participants, who then give them to the people from whom they want to solicit feedback (other approaches are included in Chapter 13). Again, whatever method is used, it is vital to caution participants who will receive the feedback not to attempt to bias the responses of their feedback sources and to assure these "others" that their data will be treated anonymously. Bosses' ratings are not anonymous but should be kept confidential, shown only to the feedback recipient. You may have to push people to respond. Timmreck (1995) points out that large companies in an upward-feedback consortium had a 41% average response rate.

6. **Process the data and develop feedback reports.** Remember, the primary concerns in this step are speed, accuracy, safety, and security. Data may be keyed into a computer, electronically transferred from computer files (the method used for the telephone-response data in the first case example), or scanned from answer sheets. Chapter 15 treats the various options available for analysis and reporting 360° feedback. Usually the feedback reports are completely customized; that is, they are confidential reports given to an individual, with his or her name used in all of the statistical report forms.

7. **Deliver the feedback reports ("cascade").** In this step, as explained in Chapter 2, feedback reports are usually delivered in a series of meetings, or

sessions, with each meeting devoted to a different leadership level. The design of these meetings emphasizes three things: confidentiality, the development of an understanding of the statistical results, and the facilitation of personal, self-directed action planning for improvements. These meetings begin at the top of the organization and work down through the "ranks," so that any given leader's manager will experience the process before the leader does.

8. **Brief the executive group on trends.** After all of the feedback reports have been worked through by individual leaders at all levels of the organization, the human resource staff studies the overall data set in order to determine the strengths and weaknesses of the leadership cadre, by level. It also looks for any other significant trends that may emerge in demographic groups. Such analyses sometimes include cross-tabulations and correlations among the survey-instrument items. As noted in Chapter 2, the trends can constitute an assessment of training needs.

9. **Evaluate the intervention.** The design of an evaluation of the 360° feedback system intervention should be approved by the executive group. Again, this may include a reassessment after a year and the development of employee-attitude-survey items that can track progress in the improvement of leadership. Persons who design and execute this type of intervention need, of course, to brief the executive group on outcomes, and in return-on-investment terms whenever possible.

These nine steps represent the basic outline of what are probably hundreds of steps that make up a 360° feedback system intervention. The major things to keep in mind when designing and carrying out such an intervention are *purpose* and *receptivity.* It is easy—and tempting—to permit the process to go off-course. The strategic purpose of 360° interventions is to improve the organization's leadership over the long term by providing its individual leaders with high-quality information regarding how they are perceived at any given time. The success of this strategy often depends on the receptivity of both the individual leader and the organization. Even the highest-quality information will not have the desired effects unless it is accepted and there is sufficient readiness to use it developmentally. The usefulness of 360° feedback corresponds to the readiness of individual leaders to use it to develop and carry out self-directed improvement plans and to the readiness of the organization to support such growth and development. Our *Organizational Change-Readiness Scale* (Jones & Bearley, 1995a) can assist leaders in determining how well their organizations are equipped to use the technology of 360° feedback effectively.

Making the Strategy Work

Strategically, using 360° feedback as a system intervention requires that all leaders be actively involved in all phases of the project. Senior leaders approve the overall plan and the survey instrument. They act as model feedback participants (authentically, of course), and they support leaders below them by providing feedback and by working with their people developmentally. As the feedback sessions cascade through the organization, large numbers of people actively participate in assessment surveys, in feedback meetings, and in follow-through on self-directed action plans.

The success of this strategy also requires thoroughness in planning. Appendix A contains a logistical-planning worksheet that can facilitate the process of anticipating the myriad concerns that such an intervention entails. Murphy's Law says that if anything can go wrong, it will. In making 360° feedback system interventions, it is vital to anticipate contingencies and to lay out a linear set of steps to be taken. Remember the Principle of Five P's: Poor Planning Precedes Puny Performance. Each step should be carried out expeditiously and thoroughly; the process of providing 360° feedback should ensure quick turnaround of results and absolutely allay any fears about confidentiality and anonymity; and data gathering, analysis, feedback-report development, and feedback should be conducted quickly and efficiently with clear safeguards for the privacy of the data.

Chapter 4

360° Feedback in Team Building

The total quality movement has stressed the importance of using data for decision making, action planning, problem solving, and change efforts. There is now an emphasis on gathering relevant information on which to base improvement planning. No longer can teams rely on "gut feelings" for direction; they must confront their members and ask "Where's your data?" Working through plans to improve teamwork requires the same standards of data. Work groups need to objectify (insofar as possible) the analyses of their collaborative activities as well as their interpersonal relationships.

Opinions, attitudes, feelings, preferences, perceptions—these are all subjective phenomena, and they can have a broad, pervasive impact on team effectiveness. Consequently, for teams to develop improvement plans, they need ways to standardize their data gathering on these psychological aspects of teamwork, that is, ways to study such phenomena as objectively as possible. The most straightforward method for doing this involves the use of survey questionnaires. This approach involves team members recording their observations on common rating scales so that their data can be combined for meaningful analysis.

Using 360° feedback in team-building sessions with groups of people who routinely work together is a delicate intervention, whether the feedback is one item or the only item on the session's agenda. It should be considered with caution, and the facilitator should develop a detailed plan for its implementation. This chapter contains two examples of actual interventions in top-level groups of organizational leaders. The use of 360° feedback in work groups, sometimes called teams, is often limited to the top level for two reasons: the work is consultant-intensive, and executives usually need to be handled in a highly sensitive manner. Often this intervention requires the use of outside consultants because internal organization-development practitioners are discounted and/or executives do not want their people to see their data.

Case Examples

The senior executives at a leading brewing company received 360° feedback that was based on two things: their individual adherence to the company's stated values and their operation as a team. The consultants solicited ratings from the direct reports of these senior leaders and from personnel two levels below them. The questionnaire was uniquely designed: it included the names of all the executive-team members, so that one form was sufficient for rating the entire team. As a result, a rater could easily compare his or her assessments of team members and note their similarities and differences.

The feedback was given during an off-site session, after about 10 hours of work on other agenda. The strategy was for the consultants to assist the team in improving its process for conducting its usual business and to build up a sense of progress before getting personal. The 360° feedback agendum focused first on the individuals and finally on the team as it was perceived by its members and others. Individual members consulted privately with one another to close any perception gaps, made personal and professional action plans, and announced the plans to the team. Then the team worked through a collective action plan for improving its internal functioning and its external "image."

One of the executives constructed an action plan for repeating the process with his own group. The implementation of his plan called for a survey instrument based on his model of leadership effectiveness. The internal organization-development consultants interviewed this leader according to our Leadership-Outcomes Model (detailed in Chapter 10). We worked with these consultants to draft a questionnaire that would meet the leader's requirements, and the data were collected. The feedback session for this work group differed significantly from that of the top team. Here the trust level was lower, so the session was specially designed to make the group members feel safe. Members seated themselves back to back at work spaces in the meeting room, an arrangement that assured them of privacy. The facilitators led them through a sample report, using viewgraphs (overhead transparencies), so that they would be able to read their individual reports when they received them later in the session. Then the facilitators passed out a sealed report to each member, asking that it be read quietly and privately. The facilitators remained in the room, available to answer any questions that individuals raised in private. After everyone had studied their statistical results, the facilitators handed out action-planning worksheets, which members completed before they left the session. The executive, who had introduced the session, then returned to make appointments with all members to go over their plans. Facilitators signaled their readiness to consult on follow-through with individual members and their subordinates.

Our second case example focuses on the senior leader of a community college who had gone through 360° feedback as part of his doctoral program in educational leadership. He wanted all of his top leaders to enjoy the benefits of such information for their own self-improvement, so he planned a team session that included 360° feedback. The questionnaire had been adapted from the one that his doctoral program has used; thus, he could get some comparative data on himself. After the consultants completed the data analysis and feedback-report generation, the team assembled for an off-site session. The 360° feedback opened the session, and it met with both anxiety and suspicion. The consultant and the top leader had to reassure participants that this was not an evaluation of them. The consultant worked the leader through his feedback in front of the group. This provided a model of how the process worked, and it encouraged others to become more receptive to their data. The lessons learned were obvious: don't lead with this technology in a team-building session, and be sensitive to the possibility that the feedback will be misconstrued as evaluation, particularly in educational institutions, in which grading is part of the dominant mindset. The session was effective in spite of the mistake in design, and the most threatened participants eventually saw the wisdom in receiving 360° feedback to guide their self-improvement as leaders.

A General Design

Here is a generic design of a team-building intervention that features 360° feedback. The facilitator needs to adapt this design to the exact needs and readiness of the team. It is vital that all of the planning of such interventions take place in close concert with the team leader.

Prework

Members of the team complete a self-assessment and distribute copies of the 360° assessment questionnaire to their panels of raters. In the case of a team-building intervention, this usually means distributing copies to the team leader and to each other. In addition, the facilitators interview all members of the team, including the leader, regarding the team itself, situations that immediately require the team's attention, and the session itself.

The Team-Building Session

The session usually involves two or three days of continuous interaction, often taking place during an off-site session. It is important not to think of this as team training. The session features process consultation and 360° feedback. The goals typically are internal: to improve the group's functioning as a working unit and to improve the individual members' contributions to it (see Jones & Bearley, 1994b for a more extensive treatment of how to design such sessions).

Timing within the team-building session is a critical consideration, as was learned in the second case example above. Another critical consideration is how much openness to expect and design for. As we discussed in Chapter 2, openness is not ideally thought of in linear terms—excessively low and high levels can be equally unproductive. The consultants need to gauge carefully the comfort level of the team and push 10 percent to 15 percent beyond that level. The leader is the model for this "stretching." He or she needs to show the team that candid feedback is useful and that being the target of team discussion can be healthy and productive.

Timing is important since 360° feedback requires an appropriate level of interpersonal trust. Our experience says that conducting a team-building session for the first time with a group requires about 20 hours of interaction. Less time than that usually does not produce a significant rise in trust. Accordingly, we recommend that a sequence such as the following be considered:

1. **Welcoming by the team leader.** This includes a restatement of the goals of the session.
2. **Generating behavioral guidelines.** This requires the team to reach consensus on a set of rules or guidelines for how to behave during the session, with the consultant(s) assisting in the process.
3. **Going over a summary of the interview data.** The consultant(s) briefly review what surfaced in their interviews with the individual team members. The summary maintains the confidentiality of the individuals.
4. **Developing a set of SITNAs (Situations That Need Attention).** These situations are taken from the interview summary, which may be posted as an aid to the process of developing consensus on what the team needs to be working on.
5. **Beginning the SITNA agenda.** Process consultation is provided by the consultant(s). The team works on a top-priority situation, and the consultant(s) assist them in learning about team effectiveness while they develop an action plan for the situation.

6. **360° feedback.** At about midpoint in the team-building session, the consultant(s) guide members through a set of steps structured to help them understand their feedback, to make self-directed action plans, and make commitment statements to the group regarding their intentions.

7. **Completing the SITNA agenda.** The team works through the remaining SITNAs, with process consultation provided by the facilitator(s).

8. **Reviewing team action plans.** This is a reconsideration of who will do what, when, where, how, and for what purposes.

9. **Reaching consensus on next steps and follow-through.** The team members test their understanding of what will happen next and how the team's action plans will be monitored and measured.

These steps vary, of course, from team to team, and how much time they take depends on the size of the teams, the expertise of the facilitators, the controversiality of the leadership, and the general readiness level of the group to face itself squarely.

Follow-Through

Teams do not stay "built." They regress, they fail to implement plans, they change membership, and so forth. It is important to plan for a reassessment of the 360° feedback after about a year, with a similar session design. If there is a change in leadership, a 360° assessment could be carried out on the new person after about six months on the job.

An Alternative for Self-Directed Teams (and Others)

Team Learning System (Jones & Bearley, 1995c) contains two instruments for use in team-building sessions. They are equally appropriate for leader-led teams as well as self-directed ones, and they can be used with or without a facilitator. The goal is *team learning.* The instruments are "fixed," that is, they are used as is. The software makes it easy to use them with teams of almost any size, to analyze the extent to which a team is doing the right things right (team functioning) and its members are engaging one another as team players.

Team learning is not the same as team building. In the traditional form of team building, a facilitator works with the group to clarify its charter, operating principles, objectives, strategies, tactics, techniques, and relationships (including conflict). Team learning requires this and more: it demands a commitment and the skill to process everyday events, critical happenings, and data about the future, all for the purpose of continuous improvement. A *team* is a group that has progressed far enough to be able to build on the interdependencies (the need for one another in order to get the work done) and to solve problems systematically and effectively. Team learning then can occur more rapidly.

Chapter 5

Incorporating 360° Feedback into Training Courses

Perhaps the most common use of 360° feedback is as a module in a training course. Participants complete a self-assessment and distribute copies of the feedback form of the instrument to their people, to be sent to a central location for processing. Then the participants receive and work through the feedback during a training course, usually on the second or third day. The courses into which 360° feedback have been incorporated vary widely, but they almost all deal with soft skills, or some aspect of human relations, leadership, or management. In recent years diversity training has often included 360° feedback as part of the curriculum.

This chapter illustrates the practice of using 360° feedback as a module in a training session. It begins with several case examples and concludes with a discussion of significant design considerations for using the technology this way.

Case Examples

At one large petroleum company, participants in a key-manager development program received 360° feedback on the second afternoon of a five-day course in strategic management, held at an off-site venue. These were managers who were expected to be the top leaders in the company 10 years later. They completed the self-assessment as prework to the course and distributed a feedback instrument to their bosses, peers, and subordinates. The questionnaires were returned to external consultants, who prepared confidential individual-feedback packages and an executive-summary report prior to the sessions. Approximately 120 leaders attended the course in groups averaging 30 participants each. Midweek, the senior-executive team traveled to the training site and held a dialog session with the participants regarding the present and future of the company. At the end of these sessions, individuals made commitment statements to the entire group on what they intended to do as a result of the feedback. After each session the consultants briefed the executive team on trends in the 360° feedback as well as other data gathered during the training. The 360° feedback module was rated as the most beneficial aspect of the course. The training was rated exceptionally high by participants. They had reunions of their learning teams, and they approached the facilitators to develop follow-up sessions.

At an oil-drilling-equipment company, 360° feedback was a "live" feature of a training course for senior managers. At the end of the second day of the five-day sessions, participants completed a self-assessment instrument. Then they received copies to distribute *overnight* to their bosses and subordinates. The facilitators received these feedback forms, combined them with the self-assessments, and prepared 360° feedback packages, delivered on the fourth day. The practice underscored a sense of urgency in the data, and participants saw the reward for taking personal responsibility for getting the feedback they needed to manage their own futures with the company.

The experience of embedding 360° feedback into a course for all leaders in a large telecommunications company was described in Chapter 3, since it was simultaneously a system intervention (involving approximately 3000 managers) and a highly rated course feature. The questionnaire was a unique part of the prework package for the course, Project Leadership. The instrument, in effect, was a message from the organization's cabinet that these 36 competencies were critical for all leaders in the company. If a leader wanted to stay there and flourish, the instrument implied, he or she would need to take personal responsibility for growing toward high levels of competence in the rated competencies.

The data were gathered in an innovative way that is now becoming accepted. Using a touch-tone telephone, raters telephoned a toll-free number, selected either a female or male voice to query them, inputted a code for the training participant they were assessing, coded in what data source the participant was (for example, the boss, a peer, a subordinate), and then rated the participant on a 10-point scale (0-9 on the touchpad). A computer recorded the ratings, which callers could change if they wanted to. Once a week the consultants took the data via modem from the host computer, developed confidential feedback packages for the individual training participants, and shipped them to the course facilitators. As the weeks progressed the norms for these items grew richer, and after about two months they hardly changed at all.

Facilitators notified participants prior to the training sessions if there was incomplete data—particularly on self- and other-ratings, since these are central to comparisons in the feedback reports. During the afternoon of the second day, training participants received their 360° feedback, developed self-directed action plans, and made commitment statements to their learning teams. The reaction of participants could be summarized by the comment that one made, somewhat rhetorically: "You know what you've got here? There's _cash_ in these envelopes!"

The next case example focuses on an international training-and-development company, whose first-line-supervision course incorporated a 26-item management-competencies instrument from Jones and Woodcock's _Manual of Management Development_ (1985). Participants completed the assessment on themselves and distributed copies to their associates, to be returned to the training company prior to the training sessions. Participants in the course received sharply targeted 360° feedback during the second day of the five-day session. The training company accumulated norms on the instrument for many thousands of participants, making the feedback progressively rich. Participants' managers came into the closing module of each session to stand beside their people when they made commitment statements to the entire group, making their own statements of intention to support their people in continuing the applications of the learnings experienced during the course.

At an innovative university in Southern California, students in the doctoral program in educational leadership go through a comprehensive 360° feedback experience twice, to establish and measure gains on critical competencies. The instrument has evolved into a highly interpretable one that shows clear content validity both for the doctoral program and for the leadership responsibilities that students carry out during and after the program in public and private school systems. The 360° assessments take place at the end of the first doctoral year and during the third one. Students receive feedback in small, supportive learning clusters, each of which is permanently assigned a professionally trained facilitator. Gains on the reassessment become part of the overall evaluation of the student's progress toward the degree.

At a major research-and-development laboratory in the aerospace industry, project managers receive 360° feedback from their course prework during the second day of a three-day intensive course. The facilitator for this module is the head of organization development, who worked with a team of project managers, executives, and an external consultant to create an instrument that closely fit the realities of managing projects in a highly complex, constantly changing work environment.

All paid personnel at a Girl Scouts Council received 360° feedback as part of an intensive two-day course, entitled A New Paradigm of Work, developed from the general content of Chapter 1 of this book. Their instrument came out of a comprehensive analysis of the driving needs of the organization's vision (see Chapter 14 for a discussion of distinctions between competencies, practices, and skills). The follow-through on this course included a reassessment, using the same instrument, with the same facilitator.

Design Considerations

The chief concern when incorporating 360° feedback into training courses is timing. It is critical to place the module appropriately within the larger design of the course. What the facilitator needs to do in this regard is determine the optimal point at which participants will be most receptive to the feedback, will be able to work with it constructively, and will be able to build on it within the course itself. Usually that point is not at the beginning of the course. We have found that about 10 hours of experiential activities need to precede the 360° feedback experience. That is, of course, only a rule of thumb, but it points to the importance of building a climate of trust and openness before using 360° feedback as a learning and planning mechanism. One tested method of generating trust in a limited time is to use learning teams and partners in the training design. Small groups and "helping pairs" can greatly accelerate the development of a learning climate that is conducive to self-exploration and commitment.

Here is a design of a typical module that uses 360° feedback as the major content. The facilitator needs to adapt this design to the unique requirements of his or her course and the readiness level of the participants to use such information responsibly. The time estimates are instructive rather than definitive. The facilitator should allow participants to take breaks as needed.

- Introduction and overview of the module. 2 to 3 minutes.

- Brief discussion of the hoped-for outcomes of the module; these include participants understanding the 360° feedback and generating self-directed action plans for follow-through. 2 to 5 minutes.

- Brief discussion concerning feedback as information and the differences between 360° feedback and performance evaluation. 5 minutes.

- Illustration of the contents of the 360° feedback packages, using overhead transparencies of a "dummy" participant. 10 minutes.

- Explanation of what to do (and not to do) when participants receive their 360° feedback packages. 5 minutes.

- Delivery of sealed, confidential 360° feedback packages.

- Silent, private work on understanding the numbers (facilitator available for confidential responses to individuals' questions). 30 to 45 minutes.

- Brief discussion of the importance of participants taking personal responsibility for making self-directed action plans to which they are personally committed ("So what?" and "Now what?"). 5 minutes.

- Silent, private work on generating self-directed action plans for personal and professional improvement (facilitator available for private consultations as needed). 45 minutes.

- Brief discussion of the importance of follow-through on the 360° feedback results and action plans, and closing remarks. 5 minutes.

This generic design works best with groups of five to about 24, with one facilitator for each 10 to 12 participants.

Data Gathering

Incorporating 360° feedback into courses presents particular logistical requirements for gathering and processing data. The usual method is to require 360° assessment as prework for the course, sometimes in combination with other activities. This makes it difficult to accommodate last-minute changes in course registration. Some training departments have adopted the policy of denying participation to any personnel who have not satisfactorily completed the assigned prework. This policy can make the training more prestigious and desirable if it is followed closely; the word gets around that "they mean business with this course."

At one time it became popular to use diskettes to gather 360° feedback data. The trouble was that they got lost, mangled, or delayed. The period required for gathering the assessment data could easily stretch into weeks, and security problems could emerge as a result. The practice has been largely abandoned. Collecting 360° feedback data on-line, through data networks, causes a number of concerns among training participants, owing to widespread fears of lack of absolute confidentiality of the data exchange.

One way to raise the odds that training participants will actually do the course prework diligently is for the organization's executives to "sell" the prework as both desirable and doable. Leaders need to communicate that the training is strategically important to the organization and beneficial to its people. They should hold people accountable for investing in the learning event just as the organization has done, and they should reassure participants that the prework is not trivial or unnecessary.

One major feature of 360° feedback is the comparison of oneself to the perceptions of one's boss, and it is vitally important that both parties approach the task of 360° assessment with more candor than is typical of performance appraisal. Both should be honest, since the value of 360° feedback rests in large part on the credibility of the data. Incomplete data can seriously jeopardize the quality of the learning experience that 360° feedback can provide in training courses. Facilitators need to work vigorously to ensure that the data reflect honest perceptions and that the data sets for training participants are complete before the training sessions.

One method for making 360° assessment easy and safe is to gather the data during the courses themselves, as in the case of the oil-drilling-equipment company, outlined above. This "real-time" data gathering, often carried out through an overnight assignment and with co-participant feedback, may require more work on the part of facilitators. If clerical assistants are available, they can be assigned the more routine tasks. Remember, however, that it is important to protect the confidentiality of the ratings assiduously. Another method is telephone solicitation, but this approach is both intrusive and labor-intensive.

There is a truly unique application of 360° feedback in training courses that utilizes response-pad technology. Both Option Finder (Option Technologies, Inc., 1275 Knollwood Lane, Mendota Heights, MN 55118, 612/450-1700) and CoNexus (CoNexus Systems, 3333 North 44th Street, Phoenix, AZ 85018, 602/852-0223) have personal-computer-based systems that permit a 360° assessment for an individual to be projected onto a screen in the training room. Participants then rate the individual by pressing buttons on a 10-key pad. The results for that individual then can be printed, displayed on the screen, or saved for later feedback. The approach is intensive in that the raters are face to face. The fear of exposure can be exceptionally high, but the sense of immediacy can be compelling.

Chapter 6

Assessing Training Needs with 360° Surveys

Using 360° feedback for assessing training needs offers a number of benefits over the usual methods of anonymous surveys, interviews, focus groups, and the like. The 360° feedback method is preferable for the following reasons:

- Potential trainees invest significantly in the process of determining what development they need and want. They are more likely to be receptive to, and actually use, the training that they influence.

- People who support potential trainees invest in identifying the trainees' developmental gaps and, as a result, are more likely to assist in the transfer of training to the job and to careers.

- Although the self-assessment of training needs can motivate potential participants, such perceptions need to be validated by people who observe, on a daily basis, the on-the-job behavior of potential trainees.

- "Two heads are better than one." In this case, many heads are better than one. Studying broad trends in 360° feedback can result in more accurate data than simply taking one person's word for what development is needed.

- Trainees follow through more thoroughly on training that they see as directly related to their chances of getting ahead. They need to be able to influence what they learn, how they learn it, and how they apply it to the job and to their careers. Using 360° feedback helps potential trainees empower themselves to use training strategically, not simply to "collect coupons."

The traditional form of training-needs assessment most often consists of conducting an anonymous survey of potential participants, sometimes including their bosses. These surveys often get low response rates, and respondents usually do not get any feedback from them. Almost never do HRD departments conduct studies to determine the extent to which the respondents are truly representative of the intended training population. The needs that surface are often highly predictable, and the process of identifying them is flawed by poor design and execution.

Here are approaches that human resource professionals can use to identify the content of training-needs assessment, or the measurement of developmental gaps, among employees (Jones & Woodcock, 1985):

- **Organizational analysis.** This entails a study of what the organization needs from its leaders, managers, supervisors, professionals, and support personnel in order to carry out its mission, attain its goals, and realize its vision. This study usually focuses on needed competencies, skills, knowledge, behavioral practices, values, traits, and attitudes that are deemed critical for the long-term success of the organization.

- **Job analysis.** This is a study of the unique requirements of a job or a family of jobs. The research concentrates on needed skills, competencies, and knowledge critical to success on the job. An assumption behind this approach is that the jobs make sense, which they often do not.

- **Model-based training-needs assessment.** This means working from an established model or one that is developed especially for the organization, showing the critical skills, competencies, and so forth, that the needs assessment must measure.

In comprehensive training-needs-assessment initiatives, a combination of these three methods usually generates the content that is most valid for the particular organization's development goals. The results of these analyses lead to an attempt to measure the present status of potential trainees to the identified content. Three common methods are outlined below.

- **Self-perceived needs.** This method is the most common one. It entails gathering information from potential trainees on what they need help with in their work. This practice is motivating, particularly if trainees are able to see their priorities in the training that is eventually offered.

- **Supervisor-perceived needs.** Some organizations have solicited needs assessments about potential trainees from their bosses. This practice can lead to misleading results, especially when supervisors are not trained in observation or have little or no opportunity or inclination to observe their subordinates and rate them honestly.

- **Diagnostic 360° assessment.** This practice requires gathering data from potential trainees, their bosses, peers, subordinates, customers, and others. These targeted individuals then receive confidential feedback and use the data for their own self-development. The overall trends for groups of employees become the basis for studying developmental gaps.

Perhaps the most promising approach is to use mixed methods as the basis for assessing training needs. It is important to reflect on the fact that such data gathering is an intervention itself, and it can have effects on everyone involved as well as the organization. The method of using 360° assessment is probably the most robust, and it has the advantage of providing higher reliability and validity (see Chapter 18).

Case Examples

In California, school administrators who apply for what is termed a "second tier" credential must demonstrate competence in several areas. At least one higher-education institution that prepares administrators for that credential routinely uses 360° assessment at both the beginning and the end of the academic program (beyond the master's level) to provide evidence of proficiency in the required competencies. Other schools are considering the use of this technology for the same purpose. The Southern California university program referred to in Chapter 5 incorporates 360° feedback early and late in its doctoral program in educational leadership.

At a major toy-manufacturing company, there was a need to isolate the competencies required to head the major profit centers and to assess the developmental needs of personnel likely to qualify for these positions in the future. The goal was to put a number of "high potential" people on track to head parts of the business after concentrated development. We began with a survey of the entire executive team to find out what competencies and qualifications such personnel need. The original instrument contained 86 competencies, and respondents could add others. This process was iterative, the feedback delivered to the executive team after each of two rounds before determining the final set. The model that emerged became the basis for 360° assessment and feedback for all potential candidates. They used the data both for career planning and establishing self-directed action plans for competency development. The questionnaire was, in effect, a strong message from the executive team that to succeed in the organization senior managers had to have the competencies and background that the instrument measured. The analysis of trends across the entire group of potential applicants provided solid information on what training opportunities needed to be created and strengthened.

Organizational Universe Systems offers a unique service, **One-on-One,** that provides intensive, well-rounded guidance to individual managers and executives on an on-demand basis. It is a kind of coaching/counseling/consulting experience that organizations use with key personnel, some of whom may be causing problems in the workplace because of difficulties with interpersonal relationships or personal productivity. We routinely use a 360° feedback instrument as part of the prework: the recipient distributes the comprehensive questionnaire to a panel of people familiar with his or her work; then these forms are returned to us for processing. The recipient comes to San Diego and undergoes a thorough one-on-one session that focuses on competencies, skills, traits, attitudes, relationships, career plans, and total life situation. The process generates a concrete action plan that includes the step-by-step development of critical competencies as well as strategies for managing self and relationships. The 360° feedback provides the core data for determining these developmental needs.

Providing the Feedback

Chapter 16 includes numerous things to consider when planning sessions in which potential trainees receive 360° feedback. In the special case in which 360° feedback becomes the basis of training-needs assessment, these sessions sometimes have a slightly different focus. Here the emphasis is on helping participants to make sense out of their data and to consider training as an attractive option for getting the developmental help that they need. In other words, training is highlighted more in this application than it might be in the type of system intervention discussed in Chapter 3.

Facilitators of 360° feedback sessions that focus on training needs must prepare to present the training options available to participants. They may also use the sessions to solicit interest in these training options, perhaps even enrolling participants in courses as part of the experience.

Participants in these sessions receive confidential, personalized 360° feedback packages and work through them systematically, concentrating on how training can assist them in meeting their career goals and doing their present jobs more effectively. The statistics may include normative comparisons, in which the individual participant can see how he or she compares with relevant groups inside and outside of the organization. The takeaways from these sessions include the 360° feedback report; information about training opportunities, including the training function's plans to develop further training in the future; and self-directed action plans for development.

Training-needs assessment is a natural spin-off of system interventions, as pointed out in Chapter 3. The cascade strategy for implementing 360° feedback provides a training-needs analysis by organizational level. Training needs can also be assessed through items embedded in employee surveys (see Chapter 7), through "smile sheets" that are used as end-of-course assessments, and through follow-up surveys on the application of training back on the job.

Chapter 7

Embedding Upward Feedback into Employee Surveys

Sometimes it is unfeasible to engage all supervisory personnel in 360° feedback initiatives. Budget restrictions, lack of readiness, time constraints, or similar obstacles may offer compelling reasons for finding a way to limit the scope of such an undertaking yet still produce highly beneficial results. One method is to *simulate* a full-scale initiative through the use of what we term "90° feedback," a strategy which "plants a seed" that may germinate into a fully developed 360° feedback intervention. Using the 90° feedback method involves placing upward-feedback items into large-scale organizational surveys; then supervisors, managers, and executives receive anonymous feedback on how they are perceived by their subordinates. This practice is cost-effective, since it involves only a limited number of items included in "climate," "culture," and "attitude" surveys that are likely to be routinely administered to all employees anyway. The benefit can be dramatic. "The attraction of subordinate feedback is in its alleged power to spur change" (Lee, 1990, p. 30). Managers like the practice so long as the data are theirs alone and are not used to evaluate their performance. Carew (1989, p. 26) says, "While we don't necessarily advocate a formal system by which salespeople or other subordinates evaluate their managers, we do recommend that managers seek out and make use of regular feedback on their performance from the people they manage."

Employee surveys pre-date 360° feedback initiatives by many years. They are an established part of organizational-improvement efforts in all large organizations, and smaller ones use them as well. Embedding upward feedback into these forms is a simple practice. It does, however, add considerable heat to the feedback process, which must be redesigned to consider the boss' and subordinates' reactions.

Some Simple Methods

Our companion book, *Surveying Employees* (Jones & Bearley, 1995b), details methods for developing, administering, professing, and reporting on all aspects of anonymous surveys in which the target is the organization or some significant part of it. The notes here, which embellish that account, focus on the special case of upward feedback.

Writing the items. We strongly favor the use of one rating scale for all nondemographic items in employee surveys. It should be possible, then, for embedded upward-feedback items to be rated using the same scale as all other aspects of the organization under scrutiny. For example, if a typical item is *To what degree do you clearly understand the vision of the future of the organization?*, then an upward-feedback item might read, *To what degree does your manager involve you directly in decisions that affect you?* The same rating scale could cover both items, and the upward-feedback items could be placed almost anywhere in the questionnaire.

Embedding the items. Where upward-feedback items are placed within employee-survey questionnaires is a matter for careful consideration. As we shall see in Chapter 12, one source of distortion in ratings data is what is referred to as the "halo effect"—the tendency to rate a person the same or almost the same on all items. In the case of upward feedback, this effect may be exacerbated if all of the items about managers are embedded in one part of the questionnaire. Respondents may see the pattern that emerges in their ratings of their managers, and this awareness may affect their ratings. We favor planting the upward-feedback items somewhat randomly among the other employee-survey items, so that respondents do not link them together easily in performing the rating task.

Data processing. Employee surveys that contain upward feedback are potentially more sensitive than are ones that do not. It is vital that the responses remain secure from "prying eyes." In processing the data it is a helpful practice to draw together the upward-feedback items into one or more "indexes," or groupings of items. That practice makes it easy to separate such items for feedback purposes, so that working through the employee survey results can proceed efficiently.

Feeding the results back to respondents. We strongly favor feeding back the results of employee surveys to everyone, and we urge our clients to make the feedback system as open as possible. This means that a manager sees the results of the upward-feedback items at the same time as his or her subordinates do. They are encouraged to work through all the data, toward an action plan that builds on the survey data and to which they are committed. Such work-group meetings should concentrate on only those aspects of the organization that they can improve, including the quality of leadership behavior within the work group itself.

Case Examples

The staff organization of a major telecommunications R&D organization used an employee survey that they named "Barometer." It was a brief (15-item), all-employee questionnaire that mapped the development of the culture over several years. Leaders of the organization agreed to embed a maximum of five items that dealt with "my manager" into the annual survey. The practice was at first visibly threatening to everyone. Employees were concerned about the extent to which they needed to respond truthfully, and managers worried about how the data would be used. As soon as it became apparent that the announced purpose, which was purely developmental, was indeed true, managers began to look forward to their year-to-year comparative results. The initiative eventually led to developing a climate in which a complete 360° feedback initiative could be mounted, and its use is now institutionalized in the organization. The practice has spread out of the staff into the line organization and is deemed highly useful by feedback recipients.

The Federal Aviation Agency developed a survey questionnaire that had all employees rate their bosses on nine areas of functioning:

- Keeps employees informed.
- Tells employees what is expected.
- Asks employees for their ideas about work.
- Credits employees for good work.
- Counsels employees concerning career goals.
- Understands the technical aspects of employees' jobs.
- Anticipates and effectively plans for problems.
- Assigns work fairly.

Employees based their ratings on a 5-point scale ranging from "very dissatisfying" to "very satisfying." As a result of providing the feedback, they found that managers and supervisors "sought to change or maintain various practices and programs according to the suggestions of employees" (Del Balzo & Miller, 1989, p. 43).

Some Caveats

The practice of embedding upward feedback in employee surveys is fraught with a number of significant dangers. HRD personnel need to plan and execute this practice carefully. Here are the principal dangers to guard against. Many of these phenomena can arise in any type of 360° feedback initiative.

Data overload. Some leaders find that the process of receiving data on themselves is stressful. It is important to limit the amount of work-group time that focuses on the behavior of the leader and instead concentrate on developing an improvement agenda for all aspects of the organization that the group can improve. The purpose of employee surveys is not to "nail" leaders but to improve how the organization functions. Keep the emphasis in balance during feedback meetings. If the leader's behavior is problematic, work on scheduling a team-building session with the group, ensuring there is sufficient time during the session to work through concerns about leadership thoroughly.

"Cheap shots." Employee surveys should not encourage respondents to evaluate their leaders negatively, under the protection of anonymity. It is good practice to avoid this possibility by omitting write-in comments from the questionnaire and by carefully working the items, focusing them solely on modifiable leadership behavior. Avoid using evaluative terms for the rating scale, such as "satisfied" or "effective"; instead, use ones that measure "extent" or "degree."

Defensiveness. It is natural for persons who anticipate receiving feedback from subordinates to be threatened by it, and it is also natural for the actual receipt to be somewhat defensive. It is critical that the process of feeding back data on leaders from employee surveys be as nonevaluative as possible. It is equally important that facilitators of sessions in which leaders receive upward feedback be acutely sensitive to this defensiveness and attempt to allay it by focusing on the benefits of using the data productively. This may require that leaders become convinced that the data be truly their own, not to be seen by people farther up in the hierarchy.

Fear of exposure. Both leaders and followers can experience concerns over anonymity and confidentiality in upward feedback. The practice of embedding upward-feedback items in employee surveys may increase this fear, since it may be widely known that the data will be aggregated into reports to the top levels of the organization. As a consequence, individual leaders and their people may be concerned about who will see the results and what may be done with them. This fear compels designers of such initiatives to make explicit the purposes of the surveys and the limits on their anonymity and confidentiality. The goal in this regard is "No surprises."

Assessment-feedback lag time. The amount of time that elapses from the beginning of the survey's administration to the feedback's delivery should be kept as short as possible. Most 360° feedback initiatives can keep this gap brief, because there is usually no compelling need to combine the data for various audiences; the locus of feedback is the individual leader. In the case of using upward-feedback items in employee surveys, it is important to plan for the prompt delivery of the feedback to individual leaders and their subordinates. When weeks and even months go by, the data become far less useful, and participants may lose their enthusiasm for, or receptivity to, the feedback.

"Witch hunts." Sometimes recipients of upward feedback want to determine who rated them at what level. Planning feedback reports should discourage the search for "outlier" ratings. We favor reporting averages for subordinates' ratings on individual items and groups of items rather than frequency counts. This practice does not tempt leaders to pressure their people to admit rating the leaders low on a given item or index.

Pseudo-evaluations of managers by executives. Embedding upward feedback into employee surveys is not the same as having employees formally evaluate the performance of their bosses. In Chapter 9 we will discuss links between performance appraisal and 360° feedback initiatives. It is important that the process of using employee surveys to provide feedback to leaders not be contaminated with appraisal. The focus here is on giving feedback for developmental purposes. Employee surveys can be used by executives to "smoke out" the less effective leaders in the organization, but this is a perversion of the technology and should be avoided. It can lead to an unhealthy situation in which the feedback is overly evaluative and not useful developmentally.

Embedding upward-feedback items in employee surveys is a time-honored practice, one that can confer some of the benefits of 360° feedback initiatives. The practice should be used with caution, however, and the feedback process should be carried out carefully.

Chapter 8

Assessing the Outcomes of Training Investments

Using 360° assessment as a means of evaluating training outcomes is becoming increasingly popular among HRD leaders. The practice involves using 360° assessments of training participants before and after instruction and comparing the results. Sometimes the design of such studies is more complex, but usually there is *no* evaluation of outcomes. Conducting pre- and post-studies of training effects seldom includes randomly assigning participants to attend or not to attend; this and other methodological problems make such research a daunting undertaking (see Miller, 1991, for a discussion of these concerns).

The foremost proponent of assessing the payoffs of training course and curricula is Donald Kirkpatrick. His model (1975, 1983, 1994) specifies four levels of measurement:

1. **Reaction.** This is the infamous "smile sheet" assessment, with data collected at the end of training. Data collected at this level are mostly critiques, and they are only loosely tied to long-term results (Jones, 1990).

2. **Learning.** Level 2 focuses on the knowledge accumulated during the training. This assessment can be made during the training itself or at the end, in the form of "tests" and behavioral simulations.

3. **Behavior.** This is an assessment of the extent to which behaviors and skills learned during the training are transferred to the job in the form of changed practices. This assessment can be carried out within a few months after the training, and it often involves gathering data from multiple data sources.

4. **Results.** This assessment centers on organizational improvements that can be directly linked to the training. This is long-term assessment, and few

organizations devote the resources necessary to implementing this level of tracking.

Level 4 evaluations are increasingly attractive to organizations that spend heavily on training, but they are difficult to carry out. Numerous difficulties in designing and executing such initiatives make them far less common than the drive for accountability in training requires. Using 360° assessments of training participants offers promise as a method for responding to this need, at least at Kirkpatrick's Level 3.

Competing Objectives

Trainers and their managers usually have different reasons for evaluating the outcomes of courses and curricula, and these differences may lead to competing objectives. Here are four potentially competitive objectives for collecting and analyzing data on training payoff, along with methods that help practitioners meet them.

Survival. When trainers are facing budget cuts, their primary motivation is to ensure the survival of the training; thus it is not surprising that the data they gather strongly tend to show positive training outcomes. One strategy for obtaining such data is to use "smile sheets," which are notorious for producing high ratings (Jones, 1990). Sometimes training departments collect testimonials regarding training courses in order to bolster their changes of survival. An additional practice is to document activities related to the development and delivery of training courses.

Course improvement. If the training staff want to use evaluation mostly to improve the present course or curriculum, they will require types of data which differ from those that support survival. Here the practice is to use "expert" judgments, suggestions solicited from various sources, and a reassessment of the developmental needs of groups of training participants.

Instructor improvement. Sometimes the objective of the evaluation is to provide trainers with feedback they can use for their own growth. This goal naturally requires an emphasis on the trainers and a method for giving them good, constructive feedback. The process of 360° feedback is invaluable in this respect. It can be applied in the form of self-ratings and -"other" ratings by training participants, co-trainers, and observers—an application that (as we saw earlier) allows recipients to pinpoint areas of needed self-improvement and to chart their progress through reassessments. The 360° process can also be used to give a trainer nonevaluative feedback on his or her training style, or manner of delivery. The feedback is solicited from training participants and others, and the ratings are compared as the trainer gains experience.

Organization improvement. Managers usually set this objective for training evaluation, seeking to determine the degree to which training is adding value to the organization. Using 360° assessment for this purpose requires an analysis of overall trends before and after training. Leaders engage in pre-training assessments, receive feedback during the training, develop self-directed action plans for improvement, and carry out these plans. After six months to one year, they repeat the process. The training staff then study what changes occurred across all groups of trainees, rather than on an individual level. The practice is not pure research, of course, since participants receive feedback, and there is no comparable group that does not receive the training or that receives some alternative treatment. This approach has the advantage of uncovering trends with some reliability, since data are pooled from a significant number of sources two or more times. The obvious limitation of this application of 360° feedback is that the links to "hard" criteria of organizational improvement are difficult to make. Someone (presumably one or more top leaders) has to decide what evidence is sufficient to justify the investment in training.

Comprehensive Assessment

The assessment of training outcomes can be conducted at several points within either a short period of time or a long one. Most people who invest organizational resources in developing people are interested primarily in producing a return on those expenditures, but often there are pressures to restrict measurement to the short term. Evaluation of training, then, depends not only on the objectives of the investment but also on how willing organizational leaders are to wait until its effects show up in the climate and productivity.

The most common evaluation points are during the training, immediately afterwards, in short-term follow-ups, and in studies of organizational improvements that can be directly linked to training. Most evaluation today is short-term, probably because that best fits the way many organizations are being managed; moreover, short-term training assessments are the easiest to conduct and most likely to produce positive results.

The very best training, of course, is tied directly to the organization's objectives and the gaps that are identified between current and desired performance. This means assessment of the participants before the training is designed, adapted, or customized. It may consist of training-needs assessments, sometimes taking the form of 360° surveys that involve potential participants and their bosses, peers, subordinates, and customers.

Using questionnaires as the basis of a tracking system. The use of paper-and-pencil survey instruments for evaluating the outcomes of training is time-honored. Trainers and administrators have surveyed participants and their people for decades. The questionnaire method has many advantages to recommend it. Here are some of the primary ones:

- **It is quick and easy.** Everyone knows how to respond, and well-constructed instruments can yield simple, direct data about training.

- **It is inexpensive.** Evaluators can amass considerable data about training on standardized, easily reproducible forms.

- **The practice can involve large numbers of "stakeholders" in providing opinions and evidence about training results.** The act of participating in such evaluations can be a form of further investment by respondents and can increase support for the training effort.

- **The reliability and validity of such instruments can be tested.** Since the method is more objective than observations, the data generated lend themselves readily to statistical analysis.

- **It can provide baselines and multiway comparisons.** Using questionnaires can enable evaluators to determine how trainers compare with one another, how they compare with themselves across courses and across time, and how participants "grow" and their performance changes.

In recent years "bottom line" has become a household term. In training we are, of course, concerned with the bottom line in organizations: the goal of long-term financial viability. Consequently, we are concerned with determining the kind of impact our work has on that fundamental goal, as well as with measuring *processes* that are thought to be correlated with that goal. This is why using questionnaires at several points in training evaluation makes sense. If we can improve how training fits the needs of individual participants and those of the organization, if we can improve its delivery and participants' satisfaction, if we can develop trainers who use each course as a learning opportunity for themselves, if we can stay in touch with participants after the formal sessions are complete—if we can carry out all of these efforts, then we can help to ensure an adequate return on investment. Using questionnaires before, during, and after training can assist us greatly in these efforts.

Here are the measurement strategies that we recommend for implementing an organizational-improvement assessment of training payoffs.

1. Administer a **culture survey**. Feed the results back to all work units, and study the overall results for training-need trends.

2. Administer a **training-needs survey**. Involve potential participants directly, since "felt" needs can generate receptivity to training.

3. As prework to the training, customize and administer a **360° feedback questionnaire** that contains items on the competencies to be covered in the training modules. Provide feedback to individuals in small groups, and study the overall data for sharply targeted training-needs assessments of participant groups.

4. Administer an **end-of-training facilitator feedback survey** by using self-ratings and ratings of co-facilitators and participants. Track courses, facilitator growth, and participant satisfaction with the modules themselves.

5. Repeat the **360° feedback questionnaire** that contains the competency items reflected in the training modules. Provide individualized feedback to participants, and facilitate their further action planning. Study the overall trends for evidence of training payoffs, and modify the training as needed.

6. Administer a **follow-up survey** on participants' self-directed action plans. Study the overall results for evidence of training payoffs, and make modifications to the training as needed. Provide periodic data summaries to senior management.

Using 360° feedback as a method for evaluating the outcomes of training investments is a considerable undertaking. The practice does, however, model accountability, and it can ensure that training curricula meet real needs, both of individuals and of the organization.

Chapter 9

Links between 360° Feedback and Performance Appraisal

"It's a nasty job, but somebody's got to do it." That seems to be the prevailing attitude toward the review of performance in today's organizations. Managers complain that the practice of annually appraising the performance of their subordinates is after-the-fact, time-consuming, and confrontative. They say there is no right way to do it—that it is a bit like going up to someone and saying, "Here's what I think of you." The basic problem is the evaluative nature of performance review, which, of course, can pose difficulties for subordinates too, such as anxiety and stress. Frequently this kind of review is paired with salary review, a practice that, in linking the evaluative material with a forecast of next year's earnings, may simply exacerbate these difficulties. The faults of performance-appraisal systems are many and widespread. Harvey (1994) pointed out four failings: (1) one appraisal does not meet all needs; (2) a top-down, single-source appraisal is inherently problematic; (3) developmental feedback given during the appraisal interview tends to get lost or overshadowed; and (4) effective performance appraisals require skills that many managers do not have sufficiently. He calls for replacing the traditional assessment with 360° data.

Almost all large organizations have experimented endlessly with their systems for appraising performance. There is the myth that if somehow we can get the ratings form right, all problems will be solved. The review *process* is less important in some organizations, it appears, than the standardization of the ratings data. Although the practice of rating the work of subordinates is inherently subjective (see Chapter 12), organizations attempt to make this top-down process more and more detailed—and thereby increasingly cumbersome. At least the more enlightened organizations are separating appraisal from salary review. Romano (1994) found that "the most common use for upward appraisals is training and development, not pay increases."

Organizations are beginning to attempt to develop team-performance reviews as well, but these schemes are no more advanced than team-based pay. Present practices still focus on employees whose bosses view them as individual contributors. And most pay systems still reward individual contributions, often at the expense of teamwork and the integration of human systems. Some organizations, however, are beginning to combine 360° feedback and performance reviews, a practice that calls for a certain degree of caution.

As our colleague Doug Watsabaugh has pointed out, 360° feedback differs significantly from performance reviews, for these reasons:

- Whereas performance appraisals are typically used to determine the rewards employees will receive, 360° feedback is used to facilitate employee improvement and development.

- Performance appraisals give employees feedback on their results—what they have already done. In contrast, 360° feedback is aimed at how they got there, how they do their jobs; thus, instead of getting feedback on their "bottom line," employees receive information on the critical skills needed for their jobs.

- Unlike performance appraisals, 360° feedback gives employees ratings from several sources, including their bosses. They often uncover differences in how these people rate them—and between "other" ratings and self-ratings.

- The data provided by 360° feedback is both comprehensive and specific. A lot of careful work goes into specifying the critical skills for jobs and the definitions of the performance levels for each.

- Through the 360° process, employees receive "normative" feedback, that is, they get information on how they compare to people in their jobs.

- Employees are completely responsible for what they do with the results of the 360° feedback. They make self-directed action plans and communicate them to others in their own way.

- Employees receive a lot of information on themselves—more than probably they have ever received before. Feedback sessions help them to make sense out of all their data and to develop their plans for improvement.

Linking performance review and 360° feedback involves using more data sources than simply the employees' managers. It requires that the review incorporate development planning in addition to making a record of employee accomplishment.

The necessity for developmental planning, which is of core importance to the effective use of 360° feedback, means that employees and their managers must approach the review process as data gathering for future performance, rather than merely document achievements after the fact. The end result of the process is a self-directed action plan, with a "sign off" from the boss, who commits to actively supporting the subordinate in the process of continual improvement on the job and in his or her career. Denton (1994) indicated that in his organization the personal-development plans are directly incorporated into the managers' appraisals.

Using multirater data in performance appraisal is controversial, and there is no credible research evidence that the practice improves the impact of the process. Tornow (1995) calls our attention to the need to determine whether linking upward feedback to performance appraisal in fact adds value.

> [R]esearch supporting upward-feedback appraisal as an alternative to traditional "top-down" appraisal lags far behind the proliferation of the method in practice. There seems to be little empirical evidence to support upward feedback in terms of improved individual performance and organizational outcome variables such as sales or productivity. (p. 2)

Further to the point, Bernardin and Hagan (1995) found that 360° appraisal did not result in improved performance, according to the supervisors of ratees one year later.

It is important to plan such applications of 360° feedback carefully. Hirsch (1994) suggests five things that the organization needs to do:

1. Establish the program's goals.
2. Decide who will be evaluated.
3. Determine whether a standard evaluation can be used.
4. Decide how many evaluations will be collected.
5. Communicate the ground rules.

It is essential that everyone understand all of the conditions of upward appraisal. There should be no surprises.

Case Example

The field sales force of a large brewing company was composed of members from 11 job families. A detailed analysis of the competency requirements of each position provided the basis for constructing 360° feedback questionnaires. The forms covered an average of 36 competency areas, with a behaviorally anchored ratings scale for each. Generally, the employees distributed these forms to their bosses, peers, and subordinates. Exceptions were made, and forms not distributed, when peers had no opportunity to observe the feedback recipient at work; also, account representatives (who worked alone) distributed forms to their external customers (beer distributors). The ratings were confidential and anonymous, except in the case of the beer distributors, who were chosen by their account representatives; they performed the ratings non-anonymously so that any problems could be addressed in private after the feedback session.

The 360° feedback was delivered in regional meetings with company facilitators. They implemented a design structured to permit people in various job families to receive feedback simultaneously. Participants worked on understanding their statistical feedback, then developed action plans. All bosses were present except for the manager above the regional manager. At the end of the planning phase, everyone made appointments to meet with their bosses within 24 hours.

Each subordinate-boss meeting had the following agenda:

1. Presenting a data summary to the boss

2. Resolving any differences in ratings between the subordinate and the boss (impasses resulted in the boss' rating becoming the "official" one)

3. Presenting the action plan for improvement to the boss and enrolling him or her in supporting it

4. Clarifying any ratings that the boss received from subordinates

5. "Contracting" for changes in leadership needed by the subordinate

6. Getting the boss' signature on a form that summarized his or her support for a concrete plan for development, including career objectives

The intervention became the basis for a completely new integration of appraisal, career development, and 360° feedback.

A Recommended Practice

If performance appraisals are so unsatisfactory, what can be done to make them better, if they must continue to exist at all? Schutz (1994) says that the traditional view is based on this belief:

> The manager works with an employee to improve the employee's performance by negotiating the expectations of employment, writing out appraisal criteria, conducting a direct and supportive feedback session, and discussing behavior rather than the person. (p. 23)

He argues for an approach that is based on the following belief:

> An employee's performance is largely a function of the relationship between employee and manager. Therefore, improvement of performance is more effectively accomplished if the relationship between the two people is improved first. (p. 24)

Schutz's focus can be illustrated by questions such as, Do we see the job situation the same way? Do we have the same goals? How satisfied are we with the situation? Working through these concerns leads to a new understanding and a kind of bonding that generates optimal individual performance.

Egan (1994, pp. 152-153) counsels managers to operate according to two principles: (1) assume that people can be creative, and (2) assume that they want to achieve more than they do, and that they think about self-development and the development of others.

The total quality movement has revolutionized the way people in organizations think about their work. Now the emphasis is on customers, even in some schools and other public agencies. A number of experts in quality have raised concerns about traditional practices in performance appraisal, even calling for its abolition (Johnson, 1990). Sashkin (1992) argues that performance review should follow, and be aligned with, a total quality effort in the organization. He advises us to "change the culture first," (p. 3) then implement a plan that has three phases: performance planning, performance development, and performance assessment. The emphasis, therefore, is on continuous improvement through dialogue between leaders and followers.

Here are some practices to consider when contemplating using 360° feedback in connection with performance appraisal.

- Prepare for change by implementing interventions that point toward culture change in the organization.

- Work toward ensuring that the accountability and reward systems are clearly aligned with the desired behavior for the achievement of organizational goals.

- Involve significant numbers of people at all levels of the organization in fashioning changes to performance-review processes.

- Consider making the performance-review process *prospective* rather than *retrospective*. Focus on planning and development, not simply creating a record.

- Consider making the process employee-driven rather than top-down. Give employees the responsibility to get the data they need to determine where they stand and what they might do to get ahead.

- Separate performance review from salary review. Make these distinct processes. Bratton (1994) spells out a method for weighting the individual's performance dimensions and attaching compensation to them.

- Use 360° feedback as the basic data set for planning development of competencies and skills. Base the assessment on ratings by the individuals being assessed, along with their bosses, peers, subordinates, customers, and trained observers (Mohrman, Resnick-West, and Lawler, 1989, pp. 94-103).

- Whenever possible, train everyone who performs the 360° assessment ratings.

- Emphasize self-management and self-leadership rather than command and control.

- Make the assessment facilitate the tracking of individual and team growth over time.

To be sure, performance review will remain a controversial topic for many years to come. Combining 360° feedback and the measurement of results to generate the basic data for developmental planning offers significant promise. There are no commonly accepted ways of doing this. The integration of these two measurement approaches requires experimentation. We are confident that effective improvements will flow from these studies.

Chapter 10

Model-Based 360° Assessment

As we pointed out in Chapter 2, one of the first steps in the 360° feedback process is to create or select a competency model, since most 360° feedback concentrates on competencies and skills. If the organization elects to use a commercially available 360° feedback instrument, the underlying model must be valid locally, that is, its contents should well match the set of competencies needed by the organization.

It is easy to become impressed with others' models, especially those that have been valid elsewhere and come with so-called "national norms." Our bias is clear in this respect. We highly recommend that organizations develop their own, unique competency models, create instrumentation that matches them, and engage in 360° feedback according to local requirements. We also believe that norms should be developed locally (see Chapter 18). In this chapter we outline procedures for developing such models, including three of our own models, any of which can form the basis for creating locally valid ones.

Why Use Models?

In our companion book, *Surveying Employees,* we point out that working from models has several advantages over "flying by the seat of your pants" (Jones & Bearley, 1995b, p. 2.1):

- Models help cut through complexity and isolate essential success determinations to be measured.

- Models can be heuristic, that is, they can lead to new knowledge and insights.

- Models help us to organize what is known into coherent arrangements.

- Models can greatly help make the feedback understandable and useful to participants.

Our experience clearly supports the practice of preceding the instrument-development phase of 360° feedback with the careful construction of one or more models that specify what is important to measure.

Developing Models from Meta-Models

A meta-model is a kind of content-free model which the developer uses to construct one from other content. A meta-model simply helps the model builder to construct other models by incorporating appropriate content. For example, the two-dimensional model that is popular in leadership-style assessment is actually a meta-model that researchers and others have used to explain differences among leaders with regard to behavior patterns. The meta-model is a grid, and the two axes are usually labeled some variation of Task and People. The underlying assumption is that the two dimensions of the grid are independent of each other; for example, a leader could be high on one and not the other, high on both, and so forth. Then the model-builder develops language for the various sections of the grid, such as quadrants. These then become the basis for developing a style inventory, or instrument.

The work of Byham and associates (1987) is a good reference for a generic listing of needed competencies for various types of employees. Another invaluable reference is Spencer and Spencer (1993).

Here is a meta-model of the model-building process (Jones, 1980, p. 172). It prescribes four phases and 10 steps:

Phase I:	*Delimiting*	1.	Observe phenomena.
		2.	Identify area(s) of interest.
		3.	Specify areas to be covered or explained.
Phase II:	*Defining*	4.	Develop salient dimensions.
		5.	Define interactions among the dimensions.
		6.	Describe the model in writing.
Phase III:	*Describing*	7.	Depict the model visually.
		8.	Test the model in a new situation.
Phase IV:	*Demonstrating*	9.	Refine the model, based on test results.
		10.	Review relationships and graphic representation.

To use the approach above to maximize the validity of a 360° assessment instrument, the developer would work through the 10 steps systematically. This would involve first selecting and analyzing the competencies—determining what competencies need to be addressed, who they relate to, how they interrelate with one another, and how they are linked to success—then developing a graphic depiction of these relationships, testing the resultant model with others for coverage and understandability, and revising the model as needed. This process ensures that the developed 360° feedback instrument is on target and that the 360° feedback will be useful to recipients.

Some Useful Models for 360° Feedback

Leadership

We developed a meta-model of leadership, the Leadership-Outcomes Model, that emphasizes the need for feedback, and we use it to uncover the theories of leaders who are interested in using 360° feedback as a developmental tool for themselves and their people. The model is a type of process flow; it illustrates how a leader's behavior flows from an admixture of personal characteristics, competencies, the broad organizational context in which the leader is behaving, and the particular situation that he or she is facing. The surrounding oval represents all of the organizational variables that influence how leaders behave. These are factors external to the leader—the context in which he or she operates and the specific situations that drive decision making about how to proceed. The **Context** is the organization itself: its internal climate; its external relationships; its purpose, mission, vision, goals, and values; its norms (how a leader is supposed to act); and its structures and systems, such as accountability and rewards. The general culture of the organization, then, heavily influences how its leaders behave.

The **Situation** is more specific: the readiness, willingness, and ability of the particular individual(s) the leader is working with at a given moment; the pressures on the leader today; and his or her goals for this individual or team right now. These two dimensions, the Context and the Situation, determine in large part what the leader actually does and how.

The Jones/Bearley model specifies two major dimensions that are internal to the leader. **Traits** are essentially personality characteristics that leaders possess. These include such aspects as intelligence, compassion, perseverance, personal values, and

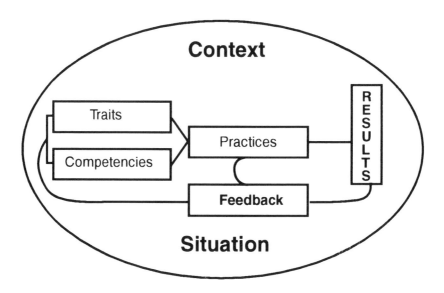

the like. **Competencies** are the developed abilities, skills, and knowledge leaders have acquired through education, training, and experience. Traits are less subject to development than are competencies, but awareness of personal characteristics can help leaders capitalize on their strengths and minimize their less effective qualities. Competencies are open to influence through coaching, training, and other developmental experiences.

Practices are what leaders actually do. The leader assesses the situation (usually quickly and sometimes almost unconsciously), reflects on what the organization needs, and takes action. What the leader does flows from his or her personality traits (e.g., intelligence, compassion, task orientation, and so forth) and competencies (what the leader understands well and/or is good at). The leader may coach, explain, reprimand, inspire, delegate, evaluate—any of countless activities. The action may or may not achieve desired **Results**, or outcomes of the exercise of leadership.

Many leaders operate in a vacuum of information about how they are perceived, reacted to, and followed. Maximizing the outcomes of leadership requires feedback that optimally guides the leader's practices. **Feedback** consists of how others perceive the leader, how they react to the leader's behavior, and the **Results** that the leader's attempts at influence generate. Developing the leader's strengths (traits) and abilities (competencies) necessitates the routine provision of feedback ("How am I doing?").

The Leadership-Outcomes Model, then, provides a way to make sense out of the available knowledge concerning how to get work done through people, how to develop them, and how to develop oneself as a leader. Maximizing results means knowing how subordinates, bosses, peers, and customers perceive the leader, how they respond to his or her leadership, and what they do as a consequence of his or her practices.

We use this model in the form of a structured interview with senior managers and executives, in order to determine the appropriate leadership traits, competencies, and behavioral practices the organization sees as critical to its success. After testing the resulting detailed model with the organization's top leadership, we develop the 360° feedback instrument and proceed with data gathering (specifications for developing such instruments are discussed in Chapter 14).

The Three-Legged Stool

Perhaps the simplest meta-model is this piece of furniture. It lends itself to depicting a condition in which three independent dimensions, or sets of competencies, combine to define effectiveness. Below is an example of three presumably independent dimensions of managerial effectiveness. The seat of the stool might denote overall effectiveness, while the three legs show the importance of managing self, leading others, and behaving appropriately within a system context.

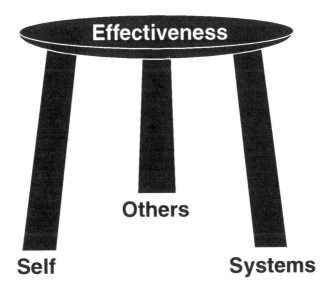

Working from this model, 360° feedback would proceed by specifying those aspects of managing self that the organization deems critical, what competencies managers must display, and what thinking, skills, knowledge, and competencies it takes to work within the system to promote the development of both people and the organization.

Working from models in 360° feedback means doing clear thinking about critical dimensions of employee behavior that are related to organizational effectiveness. When one's model is comprehensive and clear, it guides the development of questionnaires and focuses the 360° feedback for recipients. It is easy for participants in 360° feedback sessions to become overwhelmed by their statistical results. Using simple, powerful models can greatly facilitate their understanding and receptivity to the numbers. It also spells out for them what is critical and why. In a sense, 360° feedback delivers a strong message to employees about what senior leaders think is vital for individuals to develop in themselves. Their models can be graphic representations of their priorities.

Case Example

In a large brewing organization, the company's values were used as the foundation of a model on which 360° feedback was based. We arranged their values set into a concentric-circle model and displayed it graphically, as below:

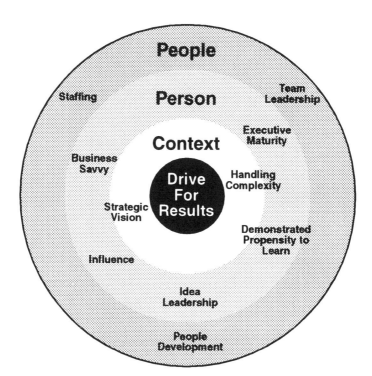

This model shows the centrality of **Drive for Results,** which is the *raison d'être* of the business. Surrounding this core competency are three competencies that focus on the **Context** of leadership within the company: Handling Complexity, Strategic Vision, and Idea Leadership. The next ring contains four dimensions that are essential to the **Person**: Executive Maturity, Business Savvy, Demonstrated Propensity to Learn, and Influence. In the outer circle are three sets of key competencies that center on **People**: Staffing, Team Leadership, and People Development.

There was no implied rank-ordering of these competencies in this model. Each set was key to the success of the company's leadership team as it worked through its people to ensure a bright and successful future for the company. Drive for Results operated as the "organizing principle," with everything around it of vital importance. Leaders needed to develop themselves along all of these dimensions.

Each dimension was described in the order that it appeared on the *Key Competencies Assessment* instrument that we developed with the client. There was a general statement about the set, followed by a bullet list of observable, improvable behaviors for each competency area that was measured in the 360° assessment.

Models can be thought of as guidance mechanisms. They assist you in developing multirater assessment instruments, and they provide ways of helping 360° feedback recipients gain perspective on the details of their statistics. Working from models is efficient in that both assessment and feedback rest on a foundation of clear, organized thinking.

Chapter 11

Using Multiple Data Sources

A basic characteristic of all 360° feedback is the use of multiple raters, or multiple data sources. The feedback recipient is assessed by a carefully selected panel of people who are presumably qualified and motivated to perform the rating task honestly and accurately. The most common practice is to gather data on leaders from the leaders themselves, their bosses, peers, and subordinates. Variations include soliciting ratings from other bosses (especially in matrixed organizations), internal and external customers, trained observers, and friends and family. Since organizations are undergoing highly accelerated change in their structures and systems, 360° feedback initiatives sometimes include people in the individual's "network," which may communicate only electronically.

The Need for Multiple Feedback Sources

Using multiple sources has a number of advantages over using simple self-assessment or one set of ratings from the boss. Although the practice of 360° feedback can be costly in terms of data gathering, the benefit of using multiple raters is effective. Here are the major reasons for including multiple data sources in 360° feedback interventions:

- **Cross-validation of perceptions.** One rater's perceptions may be seriously flawed: in self-ratings they may be distorted by the felt need to appear fully competent, and in "other" ratings, by a reluctance to be critical. Also, the rater may simply be incapable of rating self or others candidly or accurately. Using multiple feedback sources can produce trends, or data patterns, that can supply powerful information to feedback recipients. Nowack (1993) points out: "Studies suggest that in predicting job performance, self-reports tend to be less accurate than peer and supervisory reports. People may give themselves higher ratings on their own skills and abilities than others do" (pp. 69-70).

- **"Customer" involvement.** When target participants in 360° feedback interventions engage in action planning for self-improvement because of their results, they almost always have to depend on others for support in implementing their plans. Getting these other persons actively involved in providing ratings "pre-sells" them on supporting participants after the feedback. These customers of the target participants buy into the 360° process by providing their perceptions in the form of questionnaire ratings; thus, they have a vested interest in the development of the participants.

- **Multiway leadership and influence.** It is evident that even individual contributors in organizations share an interdependency with others. And every employee's behavior at work affects others. Considering the fact that leadership and influence are not the sole province of members of management or supervision, one certainty becomes clear: providing 360° feedback recipients with a balanced set of perceptual information necessarily involves gathering ratings data from representative groups of people whom the recipients influence.

- **Establishes improvement agenda.** The overriding objective of almost all 360° feedback interventions is to generate reliable, valid information that individuals can use to improve themselves at work. The desired endpoint is the creation of action plans to which participants are fully committed, with adequate supports in place for their implementation. Using multiple feedback sources makes the recipients' self-improvement a "public" agenda item. Their raters know that the goal is growth and development, and talking about the subject becomes OK. Using multiple feedback sources, then, legitimizes the topics of self-directed growth and self-management.

Self-Assessments

Rating yourself can be a threatening task, particularly if you know that you will receive feedback on the extent to which your self-assessment matches what others think of you. Probably the most significant determinant of how accurately you rate yourself is the context in which the data are gathered. If others will base decisions about your career on your results, you are likely to rate yourself inordinately high. In a banking system in which we used a special application of self-and-other assessment for 100 applicants for branch managers jobs, the average self-rating was 9.7 on a 10-point scale—much higher than boss and trained-interviewer ratings.

There is a strong tendency for people to look at their behavior in terms of required skills and competencies rather than in terms of how well they are doing (Latham, 1989). It is important, then, that 360° assessments specify that the purpose of the data gathering is not to evaluate the person but to provide information for self-development. The intervention is not a substitute for performance appraisal (see Chapter 9).

Bosses

In our consulting work for organizations, it is not uncommon for us to discover that a significant number of personnel are not sure to whom they report; often their bosses are similarly confused. This is particularly true in organizations that are undergoing rapid change, such as growth, downsizing, or other forms of restructuring. Using 360° feedback in such organizations requires that the interventionist do the prework necessary to clarify this situation. Once reliable organization charts are available, they may have to be rationalized and communicated. Anomalies often emerge during this analysis, and some further reorganization may be necessary before legitimate raters can be identified. Of course, in organizations in which people work in self-managed situations, target participants may not have bosses at all.

There are four types of bosses that may be valid sources of feedback for target participants in 360° interventions. The most obvious is the participant's **immediate superior**. This may be a first-level supervisor, a department manager, or another member of the management cadre. It is important to establish the validity of their ratings, however. Many immediate superiors do not have opportunities to observe the work behavior of their subordinates. Others may not have been in their positions long enough to provide useful information on the target participants.

"One-over-one" assessment involves the manager immediately above the participant's immediate superior. Often persons in these positions are not qualified to rate the target participants, even if they insist on doing so. In using data from two levels above, it is critical to consider the data source during the feedback process, since the data may be prejudicial and uninformed. In "flat" organizations these bosses' bosses may almost never see the target participants.

Matrixed managers can be useful feedback sources in 360° assessments if they frequently have opportunities to observe their people at work. Project and functional managers' perceptions of individuals may differ significantly, and this information may be significantly useful to feedback recipients.

One's **immediate-past boss** can often be a useful data source in 360° interventions. This person may have had a long time to observe the target participant on the job, and the ratings may be instructive to the participant who wants an accurate assessment.

Peer Perceptions

Barclay and Harland (1995) found that peer raters were perceived as fair if the colleagues were competent (educated, experienced) at the rating task and had the opportunity to change their ratings in meetings with the persons whom they rated. Although the gathering of 360° assessment data usually does not include such an opportunity, the practice of including peer ratings is common. In fact, there is a strong trend to adopt peer *evaluations* of performance as well, borrowing from a controversial tradition often found in colleges and universities (see Chapter 9).

Collecting 360° assessment data from peers requires several choices. Who selects the peers? We favor having the target participants perform this task, since the intent of the intervention is to gather data for their private use. How many colleagues should rate the target participant? Our recommendation is about six to eight colleagues, to ensure both adequate coverage and protection of the anonymity of the respondents. Which peers are qualified? We believe that target participants need to solicit ratings from colleagues who have ample opportunity to observe them at work and who are motivated to be candid in their ratings.

Subordinate Ratings

Upward feedback can be the most attractive feature of 360° assessment. Target participants usually want to succeed with the people who report directly to them, and finding out how they are perceived by their subordinates can focus their self-directed action planning sharply.

Smither, Wohlers, and London (1995) found that leaders reacted more favorably to receiving individual feedback from their subordinates than to simply being given normative feedback about how the average leader was rated. They also found that this did not necessarily result in leaders committing to change. The context of the 360° feedback intervention may vitiate the effects of gathering subordinate ratings. It is vital that the entire process of gathering data, feeding back a statistical summary, and facilitating action planning maintain the power of subordinate data.

The major questions concerning subordinate ratings focus on which subordinates should be surveyed, who will see the data, and "what's in it" for subordinates to rate their bosses candidly. We recommend that _all_ subordinates of a given manager, supervisor, or other such leader participate as raters. Failing that standard, a random selection can be made, or the target participants may choose their own raters from among their subordinate group. It seems obvious that this latter practice can result in potentially misleading data, so the feedback recipients need to be careful whom they select, why, and how they ask for participation. There should be enough people in the subordinate group to protect the anonymity of the raters, usually five or more.

Collecting upward-feedback data can be problematical in some organizations. Redman (1992) points out that unions are likely to remain suspicious of such a practice, often perceiving it as another attempt by management to marginalize them. Also, most supervisory personnel are fearful of upward feedback, at least at first, and they may need counseling assistance in accepting and working through the data.

Customer Feedback

In most cases, both internal and external customers can provide meaningful ratings data for the target participants. Since the total quality movement, many employees are aware of who their **internal customers** and suppliers are. They can select individuals from this pool of people and ask them to become raters. These internal customers may or may not be peers, although there can be overlap with that data source. We recommend that target participants who want to receive feedback from selected internal customers not choose these same people for peer feedback.

External customers can also provide target participants with highly interesting information. In a major intervention that assessed all of the marketing and sales personnel in a major brewing company (see Chapter 3), account executives, who called on beer distributors, each selected six customers to rate them _non-anonymously_. The intent of this aspect of the assessment was to improve customer relations: if any of the distributors rated the account executives low, the latter could then attempt to ameliorate the situation and reestablish a good relationship with the distributor. Everyone understood the rules from the beginning of the intervention, and the customers cooperated with a high level of participation. This practice takes courage and skill, and it can greatly enrich the 360° feedback.

The keys to involving customers in 360° feedback are customer motivation, opportunity to observe target participants, and certainty of confidentiality or anonymity.

Network Members

Structure in today's organizations is becoming increasingly flexible, with an emphasis on the temporary rather than the permanent. The terms "virtual team" and "virtual organization" are fast entering the standard organizational vocabulary. We consult in a large, multinational software company that has "virtual offices"—cubicles shared by sales personnel and their consultants, in which office work is completed using laptop computers. Generally, in such organizations people are expected, for the most part, to manage themselves. They must establish their own networks, which usually include people inside the organization, people in partnering organizations, and customers. Such networks may also include fellow members of task forces, committees, affinity groups, and "buddies." Tapping these networks for multiple feedback sources can result in reliable, valid assessments of target participants. Of course, such networks tend to be private and confidential, and interventionists need to respect those conditions. We recommend that in such organizations target participants be empowered to select their own data sources for 360° assessment and to solicit the ratings data through their own means. The data should be returned to a neutral third party, such as the HRD department or an outside processor, so that the anonymity of the respondents is ensured.

Friends and Family

It is sometimes desirable to include spouses, "significant others," children, and personal friends as data sources. We have heard many managers tell stories about taking their 360° feedback reports home, only to hear from their families: "They got that right!" Questionnaires that include only job-related competencies may not be appropriately used by such data sources, but ones that incorporate assessments of personal traits, attitudes, and general skills may be used by them in a valid manner.

Using friends and family as sources of 360° feedback requires strict confidentiality. Ideally, only target participants and neutral third parties should see these ratings. Everyone should know who will be privy to these data. It should be neither intrusive nor involuntary.

Observers

Some data sources are more valid than others because of their observational skills and their motivation to be honest and accurate in their assessments. Ideally, all raters in 360° feedback interventions should be trained and have ample opportunities to observe the target participants in work situations. Rater training can focus on the rating scale, explanations of the content of the rating instrument, and clarification of the purpose of the intervention.

A predecessor to 360° assessment is the assessment center. This usually consists of putting participants through a series of management and teamwork exercises while they are being observed by trained assessors. The observers independently rate each participant on a set of scales that presumably predict future job performance. The validity of these ratings has been controversial for many years, since there are mixed findings concerning its ability to predict on-the-job behavior and advancement success. Probably the persons who benefit the most from such sessions are the raters themselves. They learn how to observe accurately, and nonjudgmentally, and how to compare their perceptions to those of others without becoming defensive. This conclusion is valid: the greatest benefit to management in 360° feedback inventions may stem from training managers to observe their subordinates accurately and to rate them honestly. Applied to 360° assessment, the conclusion leads to the recommendation that, whenever feasible, everyone involved in the rating process receive special training for the task.

In summary, using multiple data sources for assessing targeted participants is far more attractive than simply using self-assessments or boss ratings alone. The time and expense involved in collecting such ratings, processing them, and feeding back the results can be effective in informing employees about where they stand and in motivating them to use the information for self-directed action planning. As we shall see in the next chapter, multiple-source data about a feedback recipient may vary, and the patterns of perception can have a strong, highly effective impact on the recipient; however, gaps in perception must be identified, and worked through, if the data are to generate the level of openness about job competencies and practices that is required to lead within today's organizations.

Chapter 12

Distortions in Ratings Data

Collecting multiple-source data on targeted participants can lead to the belief that somewhere in the mass of numbers, there is a "right" set—an objective reality about a given individual. This belief is usually counterproductive, and to be resisted, as the numbers are not the products of an exact science but of *perceptions*, nor are people subjects that lend themselves to objective definitions. Far more beneficial is to adopt and maintain the view that perceptual variations, despite their differences, work together to provide the feedback recipient with useful, instructive information. For example, if a manager's ratings of a targeted participant differ markedly from the participant's self-ratings, the feedback data on such perception gaps can help the participant take responsibility for opening up the subject constructively with the manager.

It may seem reasonable to conclude that a rating's degree of "accuracy" is commensurate with, or at least related to, how well the rater knows the recipient. Yet, that isn't necessarily so. Acquaintanceship should not be confused with the quality of the relationship, which can vary considerably among peers, among subordinates, among customers, and so forth. Psychology offers us the concept of core personality traits, of which there are the "big five": extroversion, agreeableness, conscientiousness, emotional stability, and culture (intelligence). Kenny, Albright, Malloy, and Kashy (1994) conducted a meta-analysis of 32 studies of consensus in ratings of these traits. The analysts found that consensus correlations ranged from 0 to about .3, indicating that there was no support for the contention that acquaintance increases consensus among raters of individuals.

The fact is, 360° feedback is inherently subjective, no matter how hard we try to control the conditions under which, and the forms in which, the data are gathered. There is a classic story that illustrates the point. Three baseball umpires are discussing balls and strikes. One says, "Some are balls, and some are strikes. I call 'em as they *are*." The second replies, "I agree that some are balls and some are strikes. I call 'em *as I see them*." The third umpire then responded, "You're right.

Some are balls, and some are strikes, but they're *nothing* until I call 'em." In this chapter we discuss the subjectivity and distortion that can be reflected in 360° feedback and offer a way of thinking about subjectivity—a way to "call 'em."

Rating Biases

A considerable amount of research has focused on the biases of raters. During the rating process for self or others, a number of factors influence a rater's judgment, and some of them may constitute potential sources of "error." Some people are more prone than others to exhibit biases in their ratings, yet whether this tendency is in itself an important personality trait is unclear. There is some evidence (Nilsen & Campbell, 1993) that discrepancies between self-and-other ratings on competencies and skills correlate with discrepancies on multirater personality assessments, suggesting that accuracy in self-perception is a stable individual difference. Regardless of who completes 360° assessment ratings, no amount of statistical manipulation can clean up the data, as we discuss in Chapter 18.

Here are the most common biases that people who rate themselves and others in 360° feedback interventions are likely to have:

- **Leniency and severity.** Some people tend to give self and others the benefit of the doubt and rate high. On the other hand, some raters seem to be harsh in their judgments.

- **Halo effect.** This is the tendency to rate a person the same or almost the same on all items. If a rater thinks that the target participant is highly competent in coaching skills, for example, the rater may rate that individual high on many other competencies as well. The reverse is also called the halo effect: if a rater thinks the target participant is not competent in running meetings, for example, the rater may rate that individual low on many other items.

- **Failure of discrimination: skewness.** This rater pattern is closely related to the halo effect. Skewness is the tendency for one's ratings to "pile up" at one end of the rating scale. Raters with this pattern either score all others high or score them low.

- **Extreme-response bias.** Some people who rate self and others in 360° assessments seem to have strong opinions about the two ends of the rating scale. Some raters tend to avoid using the two ends, and others tend to use them almost indiscriminately.

- **Sequence effect.** If the 360° assessment questionnaire is in print form, where the rater can see previous ratings while scoring a target participant on a given item, the rater may become conscious of a scoring pattern, which can affect subsequent ratings. How the items are grouped also can affect how a rater chooses on the scale. If, for example, all items related to communication competencies are grouped together, the rater may notice a pattern in the ratings, and this can affect how the next item is scored.

- **Contrast and similarity effects.** When rating self or others on traits, competencies, skills, knowledge, or job practices, the rater may be—consciously or not—comparing and contrasting the target participant to others in the rater's background. For example, some raters may compare leaders to the best or worst boss they ever had.

- **Logical error.** Sometimes raters in 360° feedback interventions simply do not understand the rating scale or one or more of the items on the questionnaire. That is why it is essential that the assessment instrument's contents be understandable to the rater with the lowest level of education and experience in the intervention. People will rate target participants on characteristics that they do not understand, and the resulting feedback may be misleading or worthless (see Chapter 14 for a discussion of ways to avoid logical errors in constructing 360° assessment instruments).

All of these "errors," or biases, can be minimized by training the raters. If such training is feasible, it should include a discussion of the need for candor and care in performing the rating task. Providing 360° feedback is serious business, and the feedback recipients must have confidence in the data in order to take personal responsibility for using it in their personal- and professional-development planning.

"Hard" Criteria

Even so-called "hard" criteria, often used to assess leaders, involve subjective judgments. When organizational leaders are measured "objectively," there is room for debate on how to define the measures and to determine where a given leader is on the scale. Here are some of these criteria:

- **Productivity.** An old story about an engineer and his wife illustrates the controversy here. She says to him, "Honey, I love you." He replies, "Let's begin by defining our terms." The truth is that organizations develop *operational* definitions of productivity, but they seldom apply them to individual leaders. Determining the extent to which a given leader is being productive is a judgment call.

- **Sales.** While this criterion appears to be objective ("What is this person's 'top line'?"), it is complicated by other considerations, such as comparisons with quotas, costs, and profitability. Determining whether a target participant is producing adequate sales involves pooling a number of observations and judgments.

- **Promotion.** Interview people who have not been promoted, and you will often hear them say, somewhat cynically, that people get ahead in their organizations according to politics rather than competency. Individuals may advance into supervisory positions because they are good at "working the system," not because they show promise of developing others well. Using promotion as a criterion is a highly subjective process.

- **Level.** Organizational leaders, as we frequently point out, do not get their jobs through random behavior. They engage in whatever behavior is being rewarded through the promotions and other rewards processes in the organization. Using the level of their jobs as a meaningful criterion for determining their worth to the organization can lead to numerous mistakes in judgment. Often there is a level above which employees are never evaluated according to objective data.

- **Tenure.** How long a person has been on the job or employed in the organization seems objective enough, but it can be complicated in the case of mergers, takeovers, and the like. Again, we have to agree on what and how we are counting.

- **Profitability.** The ultimate criterion in assessing leaders is whether their leadership increases the wealth of the organization's owners and/or realizes its vision over a long-term period. Leaders should be accountable for the long-term financial viability and accomplishment of the organization. But assessing profitability is not a simple matter. Are we referring to "profits this quarter"? Then the leader may slash costs, with long-term deleterious effects.

Finally, how can we link the person's leadership behaviors to changes in profitability? That is essentially a subjective consideration.

- **Cost Containment.** Assessing leaders according to how well they control costs appears to be an objective criterion, but it is easy to see that in order to accomplish this task, we will have to develop consensus on costs and containment and come to interpersonal agreement on a process of measurement.

- **Absenteeism.** What is an absence? Again, we have to define our term operationally. Sick days, personal leave, attendance at training and other events—all these can be considered absences, along with simply not showing up for work.

- **Accidents.** On the face of it, counting accidents seems straightforward. It requires, however, that we first agree on the definition of an accident. Then we have to develop a procedure for estimating (guessing) the personal and organizational impact of a given accident. This exercise is riddled with compromises and judgments.

- **Tardiness.** Being late for work is assessable, but it may not reflect what is behind the late arrival. The person may have been at work in another part of the organization or may have been delayed for a number of reasons, including being stopped by a supervisor. Here, too, we have to specify what we mean before the assessment can be standardized.

For each of these hard criteria there are few, if any, objective measures that apply in every case. Using such criteria to size up leaders is far more common than using 360° assessment methods, but it is no less subjective.

"Soft" Criteria

Organizational personnel are also assessed according to various "soft" criteria. These standards are more obviously subjective than the hard ones, and they are generally recognized as such. Here are common ones:

- **Ratings of performance.** Employee appraisals are fraught with measurement difficulties, and everyone who carries them out admits it. We facilitated a three-day off-site session for the senior leaders of a major business unit of a multinational telecommunications company. The program's announced purpose was the development of behavioral definitions of the 5-point performance-rating scale. Participants brought case data from actual subordinates, and they attempted to generate consensus on the following, familiar scale:

1. Does not meet expectations
2. Partially meets expectations
3. Meets expectations
4. Exceeds expectations
5. Far exceeds expectations

They could not perform the task; consensus was out of reach. Finally, they agreed to live with the subjectivity involved in this process and to focus an all-out effort on making the system fair to everyone. The session was judged to be successful.

- **Ratings of competencies.** Carrying out 360° feedback interventions also involves having many people make subjective assessments of themselves and others. The process is more beneficial when the organization's leaders clearly and forcefully communicate that the set of competencies is critical to the success of the organization, and when the competencies are described in ways that raters can understand.

- **Likability.** Many executives evaluate organizational leaders according to whether they get along well with others and "hit their number." Both of these considerations are necessarily subjective, and everyone tacitly agrees to live by them.

- **Teamwork.** Being a team player has become important in recent years, with the advent of flatter organizational structures and various forms of self-management. The "team player" concept is not, however, universally understood. Our *Team Learning System* (Jones & Bearley, 1995c) includes a self-and-other assessment instrument that operationally defines this concept.

These soft criteria, while obviously subjective, are nevertheless valid within organizations. They can, when properly structured, result in data that is enormously useful in informing leaders on where they stand, in making fair decisions about their futures, and in promoting culture change toward increases in taking personal responsibility for growth and development at work.

Averages by Data Sources

Conventional wisdom would dictate that self-ratings should be higher than those from others in 360° feedback interventions. Our experience strongly indicates that differences in the way that multiple data sources perceive an individual vary according to type of organization. The table below shows averages from several 360° feedback interventions in various settings. The averages are based on a 10-point scale, where 10 is high, or favorable.

Source	Consumer Products	Oil	Hospital	Educational Management
Self	8.4	7.6	7.8	8.3
Boss	8.4	7.9	8	8.4
Other boss	8.2			8.6
Peers	8.1		8.4	8.7
Subordinates	8	7.6	7.3	8.4

These findings show that self-ratings tend to approximate those from other data sources and that the rank-order pattern of average ratings by data sources varies noticeably from one type of organization to another. In a banking organization, applicants for a newly structured branch-manager position rated themselves 9.7! This illustrates that the *context* of the assessment can have a decided effect on the absolute level and pattern of average ratings in 360° feedback interventions.

O'Reilly (1994) describes the situation somewhat personally:

> When it is designed to provide information that you can use to become a better manager, scores from your handpicked pals or from randomly chosen associates typically turn out remarkably similar. But when used as the basis for performance evaluations, things change. Friends pump up your score, rivals become remarkably lukewarm, and that staff boob you keep reaming out cuts you dead. (pp. 93-94)

In other words, the *purpose* of the 360° feedback can bring biases into play and measurably alter the pattern of data (see Chapter 9 for a discussion of the special use of multirater feedback in performance reviews).

Dealing with Subjectivity

All observations about self and others are filtered through our "looking systems," and they are contaminated by our interpretation of the purpose of the assessment, its confidentiality, and many other considerations. For example, we tend to rate others more highly if we know that they will be aware of the data source. We may rate ourselves low if we know beforehand that our bosses will see the results. This subjectivity is not all bad, however, in 360° feedback interventions. What we are up to there is developing the most reliable, valid measures we can, collecting the data in the cleanest way feasible, and providing it to target participants in a way that makes the numbers useful for action planning for self-improvement. Feedback recipients can live with the subjectivity. They just want to see how they are perceived so that they can make some decisions about their growth and development.

Stan Herman (1972) said it this way:

> Objectivity is a concept
> And if I take it to mean my best attempt
> To hold my prejudice in check for just a moment as I hear
> It seems a decent thing to try. (p. 224)

The fact that there are many potential sources of distortion in the data we generate in 360° feedback interventions does not invalidate the practice. We simply need to accept that we are dealing with subjectivity, that everyone understands that we are not collecting people's fingerprints or conducting DNA analyses, and that the information we provide, and how we provide it, can be highly useful to leaders and others.

The Solution

If you can, train everyone in the ratings task involved in 360° feedback interventions. Carefully review the purpose of the data gathering, the ground rules of the assessment/feedback processes, the rating scale, the items themselves, and how to return the forms. What you want are informed, candid assessments (not necessarily evaluations), and you want prompt responses. You can control the subjectivity somewhat by using case material on fictitious people whom raters assess and then discuss. This can give you opportunities to clear up any misunderstandings about the ratings process. If you are unable to obtain commitment to such training, you must substitute written communications regarding such matters to every rater.

Chapter 13

360° Survey-Feedback
Logistical Planning

The Principle of Five P's—Poor Planning Precedes Puny Performance—may be somewhat of an old bromide, but it is still a good reminder of a basic prerequisite of 360° feedback interventions: thinking through as many details of the intervention as possible before taking action. A slogan on one of our office coffee cups warns: "Poor planning on your part does not necessarily mean an emergency on my part." To minimize the possibility of emergencies on the part of interventionists, this chapter lays out a five-step method for planning 360° assessment and feedback. Because the method is closely tied to the logistical-planning worksheet in Appendix A, users of this guidebook should study that reproducible document carefully as they work through this chapter.

Steps in Planning for 360° Feedback Interventions

The five-step planning method, presented and discussed below, will yield the best results when used in conjunction with the logistical-planning worksheet. Employ this worksheet in the following way: first, make copies of the form and distribute them to the members of the team or steering committee who will be overseeing the intervention's development; next, discuss the questions on the worksheet with members of the senior executive team. If you are planning a system intervention, an intervention using upward feedback, or a performance appraisal (discussed in Chapters 3, 7, and 9, respectively), use the worksheet to prepare a proposal to the top-level team. In this way, the following steps will work more effectively to ensure a successful intervention.

1. **Get executive buy-in and direction.** For any sizable intervention that uses 360° feedback, it is vital to get the active participation and support of the senior organizational leaders. This includes their completing 360° self-assessments and "other" assessments of subordinates and one another, their receiving feedback based on those assessments, and their modeling the action-planning process described in Chapter 16. The survey questionnaire should represent their best collective judgment of what traits, competencies, or behavioral practices are needed by the organization's people to actualize the leaders' vision of a desirable, doable future for the organization and all its members. Make a formal proposal that describes the intervention purpose and methodology, and negotiate their strategic involvement in the process of planning and implementing the 360° feedback.

2. **Establish a steering committee.** The intervention should not be considered a project of the HRD function. Human resource professionals should _facilitate_ the intervention, not take responsibility for its success. Such interventions should serve the attainment of the organization's goals, for which organizational leaders are responsible. Accordingly, our experience leads us to recommend strongly that 360° feedback be driven by those organizational leaders. A detailed description of such a task force appears in our companion volume, _Surveying Employees_ (Jones & Bearley, 1995b). It is easy to adapt the information provided there to the 360° feedback process.

3. **Timeline.** A critical part of logistical planning for 360° feedback interventions is the development of time estimates for each step in the process. These estimates should be based on a realistic consideration of the time needed to complete each step. A chart for this purpose is included in the logistical-planning worksheet. Teams may also use computer software to develop PERT diagrams (Program Evaluation and Review Technique), "critical paths" that show what steps must be completed before others are started. A simple chart, such as the one in the worksheet, usually suffices to brief the senior leaders on the timeline. It is important to build "fudge factors" into the plan, since Murphy's Law, "If anything can go wrong, it will," is likely to apply to such interventions.

Approximate Times Required in 360° Feedback Interventions	
Executive input to instrument	3-5 days
Data gathering in meetings	2 hours each
Feedback meetings	3 hours each
Executive briefing on trends	1 hour
Executive briefing on evaluation	1 hour

4. **Making a contingency diagram.** To have a quality-improvement tool that facilitates and structures the analysis of what could go wrong, construct a diagram such as the following:

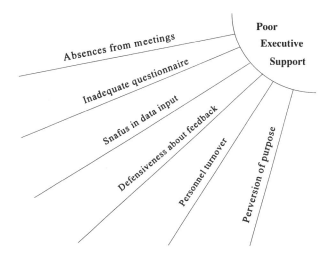

5. **Developing preventive strategies.** Develop one strategy per likely contingency. For each contingency identified in step 4, develop a prevention checklist. The chart below illustrates one such list. What you are doing in steps 4 and 5 are anticipating what could go wrong in your 360° intervention and devising strategies and tactics to ensure success. Below is an example of a preventive strategy for poor executive support.

Poor Executive Support
Strategy
• Involvement in instrument development • Approval of intervention strategy • Presentations in meetings • Modeling action planning themselves • Cover letters on questionnaires

Special considerations must be taken into account. These include holidays, planned organization events (especially ones announcing layoffs, stock splits, and the like), and vacation periods.

It is often observed that planning is easier than implementation. It is important to expect that any application of 360° feedback will be accompanied by unforeseen difficulties. Some of these can be prevented, but others need to be adapted to. The consideration that you need to keep central is the purpose of the intervention. Involving key personnel in the planning process begins with developing a common commitment to why the intervention is desirable. Then this group can make proper adjustments to the inevitable contingencies.

Chapter 14

Creating 360° Assessment Instruments

The measurement device that forms the basis for multirater feedback is of critical concern. In this chapter we spell out our experiences and points of view regarding several dimensions related to instrumentation. We will discuss how to ensure that the content is valid, that the rating scale is appropriate, that the format of the questionnaire makes it easy to complete, and that the instrument has an appropriate appearance.

There is no way to recover from using a faulty instrument; no amount of statistical or verbal manipulation will make the resultant feedback work. While it is tempting to use off-the-shelf instruments that *appear* to be reliable and valid, we strongly contend that it is almost always preferable to develop instruments that sharply target the organization's and participants' unique needs. Hence the necessity for focusing our attention on how we construct multirater instruments.

Published instruments can be useful sources of information on how to go about the task of developing such questionnaires. One classic source is Morrison, McCall, and DeVries (1978; for an update of this work, see Velsor & Leslie, 1991a and 1991b). Developers can see how others have formatted their questionnaires, what content they have included, what rating scales they employ, and so forth, as ideas for adaptation to local conditions and needs.

The Content of the Instrument

When developing a 360° assessment questionnaire that focuses on leadership, you will need to ensure that its content aligns clearly with the organization's purpose, mission, and vision. If the instrument focuses on quality behaviors, for example, you may have to develop content that will produce reliable feedback on the critical behaviors found by the organization to be directly relevant to its emphasis on quality.

It is important that whatever the instrument covers, the items themselves be ratable. It is unlikely that raters will know the extent to which the individual being rated trusts others; nonetheless, they will rate the item anyway. Then you will have loose, inferred, contaminated ratings that may not be useful for developing feedback.

It is equally important that the content of the questionnaire center on personal characteristics that the feedback recipient can develop. In other words, the usual overarching purpose of the measurement and feedback is to provide solid data to the recipient in order to facilitate action planning for improvement. Telling a person "Your average rating on having nervous twitches is 5.4" may actually be damaging instead of informative. The items must be about what the individual can do something about.

The instrument must appear valid to respondents, that is, everyone who performs the ratings needs to feel that the questionnaire makes sense. In practice, this requires that the language used in the instrument reflect that of the raters, that the content be obviously relevant to them, and that the instrument hang together well.

It is tempting to measure too many things in multirater feedback instruments. Brevity is a critical requirement for such assessments because of two primary factors: (1) the need for raters to complete the task quickly, and (2) the necessity that the feedback be completely understandable to the feedback recipients. We recommend that 360° assessment instruments contain less than 50 items, and that they contain no demographic scales (e.g., gender, age, tenure, level).

Item Criteria

For instrument items to be useful, they must be constructed carefully. A simple way to test each of your items is to ask if the item can be described as the following:

- **Unidimensional.** This means that the item measures only one thing. Perhaps the most common survey-item error is the double question, for example, "To what extent does this person coach and counsel subordinates effectively?" Coaching and counseling are two different activities, of course, and they require separate measurement. The item should be recast as two; otherwise, how does the rater respond if the person being rated is effective on one but not the other?

- **Free of qualifiers.** Words like "usually," "always," "never," and "good" can invalidate the rating scale. For example, if you use a "Strongly agree—

Strongly disagree" rating scale, and an item reads, "This person always involves others in decisions that affect them," how would a rater respond if the person being rated *sometimes* does this, but not *always*? Such qualifiers should simply be eliminated.

- **Observable.** The rater must have had the opportunity to see what is being rated. Asking raters to infer and judge is asking for contaminated data. The item, "To what degree is this person skilled in making his or her points clear under stress?" is preferable to "To what degree is this person good at handling conflict situations?" The former can be directly observed, whereas the latter represents an inference or summary judgment. The difficulty with items that require inferences and judgments is that raters will respond to them, but the recipient of the feedback may not be able to interpret the data or find ways to improve on those items.

- **Tied to the scale.** If you use a frequency scale, the items must be written to conform to it. The item "This person shows competency in being able to locate prospective customers effectively" requires a *degree* scale rather than a rating of frequency.

- **Clear and understandable.** Ideally, every rater needs to interpret each item the same way. That means avoiding any language that is ambiguous, jargonistic, or at too high a level of comprehension. Good rules are to use easy, common words and to write at the lowest educational level of the personnel who will respond to the instrument.

- **Ratable by the data sources.** Since 360° feedback interventions often involve such disparate sources of ratings as self, bosses, peers, subordinates, internal customers, external customers, trained observers, and friends and family, it is critical that the items cover what these raters know something about; otherwise there will be many holes in the feedback. Our practice is to determine the sources of ratings before constructing the instrument, so that we include only those items that respondents are qualified to rate.

- **Developmental ("So what? Now what?").** Instrument items should center on things that the feedback recipient can do something about. The goal is to generate reliable, valid data that will be useful for developing self-directed action plans for improvement. Getting feedback on "To what degree does this person display an attitude of optimism?" would probably not be so useful to feedback recipients as one that asks, "To what degree is this person able to assist you in analyzing your problem situations at work?"

- **Aligned with the organization's vision.** The item set should concentrate on what is critical to realizing the hoped-for future of the organization. The connection between what the instrument measures and what the organization stands for and is headed toward should be obvious to all respondents. In a sense, 360° feedback instruments are strong organizational messages about what is important: "If you're going to stay here and flourish, you need to become highly competent in these areas." This approach obviates the need for "importance" ratings; every item has already been decided to be critical to carrying out the organization's intentions.

Content Areas

Developing instruments for 360° feedback entails choosing appropriate content. The steps for conducting 360° system interventions, outlined in Chapter 3, include the specification of needed competencies in an organization. If you choose to measure other dimensions of individuals, here are categories to consider:

- **Skills:** Sets of behaviors that are shaped toward "objective" standards.

  Examples: designing meetings, writing objectives, listening, repairing a machine.

- **Competencies:** Developed abilities. Competencies are more general than skills, and often subsume sets of skills.

  Examples: intervening in conflict situations, providing performance feedback, elucidating vision, strategic planning.

- **Traits/Characteristics:** Descriptions of the feedback recipient as an individual—his or her "character."

  Examples: trustworthiness, intelligence, creativity/innovativeness, decisiveness.

- **Attitudes/Feelings:** Inferred from behavior. Attitudes are predispositions to behave predictably toward an object or class of objectives. Feelings are emotions that are experienced in reaction to, or anticipation of, situations and events.

  Examples: "isms," optimism, patience, anger.

- **Behaviors/Leadership Practices:** Observable: what the person actually does.

    Examples: involving people in planning, interceding for subordinates, making "command" decisions, expressing caring.

Again, it is important to concentrate the items on what the feedback recipient can improve, since that is the usual overriding consideration in such interventions.

Rating Scale

All of the items on the instrument should be rated according to the same scale. This practice makes it easy to compare data among items, and it avoids confusing raters. The choice of which rating scale to use is not simple, however. You should consider organizational custom (the scales normally used in this organization), whether to use even- or odd-numbered scales, the ability of respondents to make distinctions, and whether you need respondents to be descriptive or evaluative.

Many organizations traditionally use 5-point rating scales on almost all instruments. This practice can lead to quibbling over the midpoint of the scale and to confusion about meaning in feedback sessions. We favor the use of 6- and 10-point scales for 360° assessment instruments. Raters have to "lean one way or the other," the scales are wide enough to be sensitive to year-to-year development, and raters can almost always make the distinctions that the scales require.

Importance ratings and other double scales can overload feedback recipients. We strongly recommend that 360° assessment instruments contain only critical content and that raters simply assess the individual on those items. The goal here is not to discover what is important; that is a task that must be accomplished before constructing the instrument. The goal is to provide clear, simple, easy-to-understand data summaries to feedback recipients so that they can make self-directed action plans for improvement.

Here is a representative sample of some common forms of rating scales used in 360° assessment instruments. These scales appear in commercially available 360° assessment questionnaires.

RECOMMENDED TYPES OF RATING SCALES

10	Definitely like this person	5	Somewhat like this person
9		4	
8	Like this person	3	Unlike this person
7		2	
6	Somewhat like this person	1	Definitely unlike this person

10	High	5	Medium
9		4	
8		3	
7		2	
6	Medium	1	Low

7 = To a very great degree	3 = To a little degree
6 = To a great degree	2 = To a very little degree
5 = To a moderate degree	1 = Not at all
4 = To some degree	

Very satisfied	Dissatisfied
Satisfied	Very dissatisfied
Somewhat satisfied	Not applicable
Somewhat dissatisfied	

1 = Very weak (bottom 5%, compared to others at his/her level

2 = Clearly below average (next 10%)

3 = Somewhat below average (next 20%)

4 = Typical (middle 30%)

5 = Somewhat above average (next 20%)

6 = Clearly above average (next 10%)

7 = Outstanding (top 10%)

DK = Don't know

1 = Very limited extent, Never, or Not at all

4 = Average extent, About normal in degree or frequency

7 = Very great extent, Always, or Without fail

RECOMMENDED TYPES OF RATING SCALES	
6 Almost always 5 Frequently 4 Usually	3 Sometimes 2 Infrequently 1 Almost never
C = Completely true M = Mostly true S = Somewhat true	L = A little true N = Not at all true
4 = Extremely effective (very satisfied) 3 = Very effective (fairly satisfied) 2 = Effective (neither satisfied nor dissatisfied) 1 = Only slight effective (somewhat dissatisfied) 0 = Not effective (very dissatisfied)	
1 = Rarely or never 2 = Once in a while 3 = Sometimes	4 = Fairly often 5 = Very frequently or always
4 = Always 3 = Regularly	2 = Sometimes 1 = Rarely
0 = Never 1 = Rarely 2 = Sometimes	3 = Frequently 4 = Always
5 = Among the best 4 = Better than most 3 = Adequately	2 = Less well than most 1 = Among the worst
Strongly agree Agree Hard to decide	Disagree Strongly disagree
1 = Extremely poor 2 = Below average 3 = Average 4 = Above average 5 = Excellently	NEI = Not enough information N/A = Not applicable

RECOMMENDED TYPES OF RATING SCALES

4 = Usually, to a great extent   NA = Not applicable 3 = Sometimes, to a moderate degree   DK = Don't know 2 = Seldom, to a small extent 1 = Never, not at all
Agree   ?   Disagree
Essentially unlike you Like you quite often Like you most of the time
0 = Rarely   1 = Sometimes   2 = Often
True False

Behaviorally Anchored Rating Scales

There is a special kind of rating scale that is sometimes used in 360° assessment instruments. BARS, or behaviorally anchored rating scales, feature detailed descriptions of their scale points. The following example of such a scale comes from a set of 11 job-specific questionnaires we developed for the sales and marketing function of a large brewing company (see Chapter 3).

INTERPERSONAL

SKILL DESCRIPTION: Develops and maintains a friendly rapport with others; demonstrates a sensitivity to their feelings; respects the dignity of others and responds with empathy to their own sense of self-worth.

Ratings 1 and 2: Demonstrates the ability to get along well with subordinates, managers, and peers; strives to achieve work group objectives. Can express own ideas, thoughts, and feelings and considers the needs, ideas, and feelings of others.

Ratings 3 and 4: Demonstrates the ability to apply factors of effective listening, on a one-to-one basis, such as displaying interest, not interrupting when another is speaking, and withholding judgments. Consistently provides honest (both positive and negative) feedback and provides constructive criticism when appropriate.

Ratings 5 and 6: Demonstrates the ability to consistently consider and respond to the needs and ideas of others which encourages and stimulates further communication. Effectively listens in group or one-to-one situations involving distractions, stress, complex information, or when the person speaking is emotional/distraught. Creates/maintains a positive working environment that encourages expression of thoughts, ideas, and feelings.

Since all of the rating scales that appear above are used in widely distributed, commercially available instruments, it seems obvious that there is no one best scale for use in 360° assessment instruments. Developers need to study these scales carefully and adapt them to their particular interventions.

Write-In Comments

Timmreck (1995) indicated that 52% of members of a consortium of large companies included write-in comments on their multirater questionnaires (see Chapter 1 for more information on this consortium). Our experience is that the inclusion of this feature greatly complicates the development of feedback reports and that feedback recipients appreciate the information. Our recommendation is that you limit such comments to suggestions for improvement and limit raters to only one comment or suggestion. You could word the item something like this:

> *In the space below, write one suggestion for improvement for this person. Please write legibly, and limit yourself to one suggestion. These will be combined into a report for the person whom you rated.*

The Format of the Instrument

Instruments for 360° assessment can take several forms, both print and electronic. The most common one is "paper and pencil," or printed forms. Sometimes these instruments can be complicated, especially when they contain demographic items and special instructions. Our preference is to have the questionnaire printed on one side of one page and, if possible, in a scannable mode. The instructions should be simple and absolutely clear, and the respondent should be able to mark ratings directly on the form. Also, it is important to adopt a comfortable way that the respondent can return the form to a credible place or person, that is, a way that poses no threat to the experience of performing the ratings task.

With the advent of computer networks and electronic mail, a number of organizations have experimented with electronic data gathering. This can add considerably to respondent's fear of exposure, so the practice must be planned extremely carefully. Raters need to trust that their data will remain anonymous (usually a concern of peers and subordinates) and confidential (for example, in the case of self and bosses). While Edwards (1994) indicates that respondents complete the ratings task about 40% faster on screen, Timmreck (1995) indicates that only about 7% of large companies use this medium for collecting 360° feedback ratings.

While it is technically feasible to gather 360° assessment data over computer networks or telephone lines, it is vital to develop this aspect of your intervention extremely carefully, to ensure adequate and appropriate participation. In one such survey, the organization's human-factors engineers studied the system before it was implemented.

The Appearance of the Instrument

Your instrument should look professional and nonthreatening. It should be reproduced to appear neat and well organized. The form should have a "typeset" look, and it should incorporate the organization's image in the form of a logo and perhaps a motto as well.

People who receive the instrument should be motivated to complete it immediately and carefully. The person who is being rated should be clearly designated, and it should be easy for respondents to indicate how they relate to this person. They should be able to change their responses easily, and they should get clear instructions on how to return the form.

This chapter has laid out a number of technical considerations in developing 360° assessment instruments. It is important to reflect on the need for thoroughness and care in this task. There is an old computer-world acronym: GIGO, or Garbage In, Garbage Out. In other words, if you have a poorly constructed questionnaire, the results are likely to be of only limited usefulness. We have a further warning: GITO, or Garbage In, Truth Out. People tend to believe what comes out of computers. Feedback recipients can be misled by feedback from faulty instruments. The fact that the data have been statistically analyzed and perhaps displayed in attractive graphics says nothing about the usefulness of the results. Poorly developed 360° assessment instruments can cause feedback recipients to draw erroneous conclusions about themselves. Care in developing such questionnaires is an ethical imperative.

Chapter 15

Data Analysis and Reporting

You have administered your 360° assessment survey, and the returns are coming in. Now it is time to get the ratings into an electronic form that makes it possible to analyze them and develop feedback reports for recipients. In this chapter we will discuss a number of practices to consider when processing data and developing feedback reports.

Data Input and Analysis

The most common forms for inputting 360° ratings into computers for processing and reporting are keyboard entry, optical mark readers (scanned answer sheets, usually), and file insertion. Each of these approaches has its drawbacks, and you should consider them as part of your logistical planning for the 360° feedback intervention (see Chapter 13).

Keyboard Inputs. If you have a software package that can analyze such data, you can enter data directly from the computer keyboard, using the numeric keypad. This method is preferable when you have surveyed only a few people, but it is cumbersome and error-prone when used for surveys with significant numbers of respondents. We recommend that this method be used only with interventions that involve less than 25 feedback recipients. The practice that works best for us is to have two people record the ratings, one calling them out while the other inputs them. We sort the returned printed forms into stacks by feedback recipient first. We print our questionnaires with spaces between every four or five items so that this input process is easier.

Scanned Input. Using scannable forms greatly reduces the potential for human error in inputting ratings data. This method is preferable in most 360° interventions, since it is familiar to respondents, fast, and easy. You can either purchase or lease optical mark readers; the most popular models in the United States are made by Scantron and NCS. It is important to note that printing your 360° assessment questionnaire directly on a scannable form can take several weeks. Raters need to be taught how to use the forms, particularly how to mark and erase on them. An alternative to obtaining a dedicated machine for scanning answer sheets is to use desktop scanners and software that "teaches" the scanner how to interpret your questionnaire-response areas. Many of these scanners include optional sheet feeders. This method of inputting 360° ratings can be cost-effective for surveys with 25 to 100 participants.

File Input. Some organizations collect 360° assessment data through computer networks. Although we do not routinely recommend this strategy because of raters' fear of exposure, the practice is becoming increasingly common. With this method of data collection, such as through *Lotus Notes,* you end up with a computer file of numbers, including codes for participant identification, data-source identification, and the actual ratings. The data-collection package can usually export such a file in a form, usually ASCII "comma-delimited," that can be used by other applications, which you then use for preparing feedback reports. The potential drawbacks of this method of input are primarily that people tend strongly to mistrust the confidentiality of computer-assisted communications ("hackerphobia") and that files can become corrupted or even lost altogether. We recommend this method of data collection and file input only be used by organizations with reasonably open climates and in which employees are significantly computer literate.

The authors have developed a software package that is dedicated to 360° assessments and reporting. The *Management Skills Assessment System* (MSAS) (Jones & Bearley, 1994a) makes it easy to develop multirater instruments, to input the data, and to generate a wide array of feedback reports. All of the methods of data input described above work with the MSAS.

Feedback Reports

When you have entered all the ratings data, you are then ready to develop a feedback report for each individual person on whom ratings were collected. The typical 360° feedback report contains several pages of statistical results data that focus on the individual feedback recipient. These reports usually include comparisons with others in the feedback recipient's organization, and they sometimes compare that individual to statistical norms developed on outside groups.

Often the report includes action-planning worksheets, such as those contained in Appendix B. We will discuss the feedback *process* in the next chapter. Here we will briefly discuss the most common forms of 360° feedback of numerical data and suggestions for improvement.

The important thing to keep in mind while you are devising the formats for your reports is that they must make sense to the feedback recipients without time-consuming consultation. The rule is to simplify the reports sufficiently so that the recipient can interpret them without the assistance of a facilitator or consultant, even long after the feedback has been worked through. Our goal here is not to impress feedback recipients, but to inform them about how they are perceived. We are not conducting psychological research; we are providing a mechanism to make it easy for people to learn how others see them, in comparison to how they see themselves. Kahneman, Slovic, and Tversky (1982) found that the more detailed the report is, the more feedback recipients concentrate on those results that match their self-perceptions and ignore the contradictory data. London and Beatty (1993) recommend averaging items within categories or indexes, stating that doing so provides enough detail. They argue that "showering a manager with statistics makes the process potentially threatening to his or her self-concept because of the fear of negative results" (p. 369).

Common Feedback Report Formats

Here are examples of the most common formats that organizations use to provide 360° feedback to individuals. (These examples were developed by using our Management Skills Assessment System software.) The details of these formats vary widely, of course.

Items by average. This report often displays the feedback recipient's average ratings from everyone who rated the recipient, in rank order, either high to low or low to high. Sometimes self-ratings are excluded from reports like this. Sometimes the report includes the standard deviation of the ratings for each item, but we do not recommend this practice. Sometimes the report compares the person's average rating on each item to a norm group, such as everyone who participated in the intervention during the current year or people in some "industry norm" group (see Chapter 18 for a discussion of the relative merits of developing your own organizational norms and using "external" ones). An items-by-average report, then, is a type of "snapshot" of the individual's results, often all on one page.

Management Competency Feedback Survey
Summary of Item Averages (High to Low) for Pat Armstrong

Scale
    10 - Definitely like this person
    9
    8 - Like this person
    7
    6 - Somewhat like this person
    5 - Somewhat unlike this person
    4
    3 - Unlike this person
    2
    1 - Definitely unlike this person

Item	Raters	Average
31. Monitors the task performance of subordinates.	14	9.6
29. Counsels with subordinates on their personal concerns.	14	9.3
3. Gives others constructive criticism.	14	8.8
14. Helps others to develop their abilities.	13	8.5
23. Listens to others effectively.	13	8.5
32. Maintains performance standards.	13	8.5
26. Keeps job roles clear.	14	8.4
20. Shows sensitivity to others' feelings.	14	8.4
28. Gives subordinates the authority to do their work.	13	8.1
25. Allows subordinates to make decisions when appropriate.	14	7.9
10. Delegates tasks appropriately.	14	7.9
24. Has a good sense of humor.	13	7.8
6. Establishes clear job-task expectations.	14	7.7
7. Gives others recognition for their accomplishments.	14	7.7
4. Shows consideration for others.	14	7.6
9. Helps others to see the importance of their work.	14	7.6
1. Motivates others effectively.	14	7.6
8. Lets others know how well they are doing.	14	7.5
22. Expresses feelings openly.	14	7.5
11. Confronts others in a skillful manner.	14	7.4
19. Coaches others in developing their skills.	14	7.4
21. Encourages new ideas and procedures.	14	7.4
2. Explains new tasks clearly.	14	7.3
17. Adapts his/her leadership style to individuals.	14	7.3

Item	Raters	Average
5. Works well with others in setting their goals.	14	7.2
13. Evaluates the performance of others effectively.	14	7.2
18. Communicates well with others.	14	7.2
27. Uses subordinate suggestions well.	14	7.2
30. Provides appropriate resources for subordinates.	14	7.0
12. Involves people in decisions that affect them.	14	6.9
16. Organizes projects effectively.	14	6.7
15. Is receptive to feedback.	14	6.5
Armstrong		7.7
XYZCO		8.5

Strengths and needs. Isolating the top- and bottom-rated items for a feedback recipient can be an economical way of assisting the individual in working through two significant processes: claiming his or her strengths and determining what to concentrate on in improvement planning. If you restrict such a report to five or six items in each category, the statistics can be displayed on one page. This can greatly aid in the action-planning process during feedback. Normally the strengths and needs (or "opportunities for improvement") are selected according to the averages of all raters of the individual on the questionnaire items.

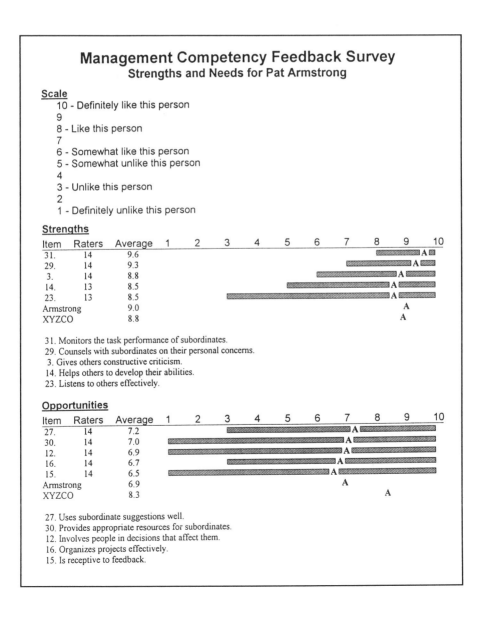

Gap. Feedback recipients are naturally curious to learn what differences there may be in how they rated themselves compared to how others rated them. Often they are acutely interested in how their bosses see them, and, if they supervise the work of others, how their subordinates rated them. A statistical report that displays the greatest differences between self-ratings and "other" ratings meets this curiosity and provides a basis for planning to narrow these perceptual gaps. Usually such a report compares self and each "other" data source separately. For example, a feedback recipient might learn that his or her self- and boss ratings differ prominently in several important areas. The individual then makes a plan to solicit more detailed feedback from the boss in order to close the gap.

Management Competency Feedback Survey
Largest Gaps Between Self and Other Ratings for Pat Armstrong

Self	Other(s)	Gap	Item
--- Self Compared to Boss ---			
10	7	3+	8. Lets others know how well they are doing.
10	8	2+	4. Shows consideration for others.
10	8	2+	7. Gives others recognition for their accomplishments.
10	8	2+	9. Helps others to see the importance of their work.
10	8	2+	11. Confronts others in a skillful manner.

Differences and percentages of paired ratings on all 32 items:
No diff: 31.3%; 1 point: 31.3%; 2 points: 34.4%; 3 points: 3.1%

Self	Other(s)	Gap	Item
--- Self Compared to Peers ---			
10	7.25	2.75+	12. Involves people in decisions that affect them.
9	7.00	2.00+	15. Is receptive to feedback.
10	8.00	2.00+	16. Organizes projects effectively.
10	8.25	1.75+	17. Adapts his/her leadership style to individuals.
10	8.50	1.50+	24. Has a good sense of humor.

Differences and percentages of paired ratings on all 32 items:
No diff: 43.0%; 1 point: 31.3%; 2 points: 17.2%; 3 points: 3.1%; 4 points: 4.7%; >4 points: 0.8%

Self	Other(s)	Gap	Item
--- Self Compared to Subordinates ---			
10	5.50	4.50+	16. Organizes projects effectively.
10	5.63	4.38+	30. Provides appropriate resources for subordinates.
10	6.00	4.00+	21. Encourages new ideas and procedures.
10	6.13	3.88+	12. Involves people in decisions that affect them.
10	6.38	3.63+	6. Establishes clear job-task expectations.

Differences and percentages of paired ratings on all 32 items:
No diff: 14.7%; 1 point: 20.3%; 2 points: 17.5%; 3 points: 10.8%; 4 points: 13.5%; >4 points: 23.1%

Self	Other(s)	Gap	Item
--- Self Compared to All Other Sources Combined ---			
10	6.46	3.54+	16. Organizes projects effectively.
10	6.69	3.31+	12. Involves people in decisions that affect them.
10	6.77	3.23+	30. Provides appropriate resources for subordinates.
10	7.08	2.92+	17. Adapts his/her leadership style to individuals.
10	7.15	2.85+	21. Encourages new ideas and procedures.

Data source summary. Sometimes it is desirable to develop comprehensive feedback reports on the entire data set for individual participants in the 360° assessment intervention. Reporting how all data sources rated the feedback recipient on each survey item gives the maximum detail that we recommend. We never show the array of ratings regarding how the individual was rated by anonymous groups, such as peers, subordinates, and customers. That practice would encourage "witch hunts," or attempts to find out who were the "ouliers," the persons who may have rated the person differently than the others. Frequency-by-data-source reports typically include, for each item, the self-rating, the boss rating, and the averages of the ratings given by the feedback recipient's peers and/or subordinates. Sometimes such reports display the items in rank order by the individual's overall averages, from low to high or vice versa.

Management Competency Feedback Survey
Data-Source Summary for Pat Armstrong

Scale
10 - Definitely like this person
9
8 - Like this person
7
6 - Somewhat like this person
5 - Somewhat unlike this person
4
3 - Unlike this person
2
1 - Definitely unlike this person

1. Motivates others effectively.

Data Source	Number	Average	1 2 3 4 5 6 7 8 9 10
Self	1	9.0	
Boss	1	8.0	
Peers	4	8.8	
Subordinates	8	6.8	
Armstrong	14	7.6	
XYZCO	311	8.3	

2. Explains new tasks clearly.

Data Source	Number	Average	1 2 3 4 5 6 7 8 9 10
Self	1	9.0	
Boss	1	10.0	
Peers	4	8.5	
Subordinates	8	6.1	
Armstrong	14	7.3	
XYZCO	311	8.3	

3. Gives others constructive criticism.

Data Source	Number	Average	1 2 3 4 5 6 7 8 9 10
Self	1	10.0	
Boss	1	10.0	
Peers	4	9.0	
Subordinates	8	8.4	
Armstrong	14	8.8	
XYZCO	311	8.3	

"Index" profile. It is common for 360° feedback surveys to include items that have been written to measure various aspects of major dimensions. For example, your questionnaire may contain several items related to communication competencies or skills. You may want to combine information from these items in a cluster, or index. This statistical report typically displays each index, or dimension, along with data from the items that compose it. Sometimes this report breaks out the information by data source, so that the feedback recipient can see his or her profile as reflected by the ratings of self and others.

Management Competency Feedback Survey
Index Summary for Pat Armstrong

Scale
10 - Definitely like this person
9
8 - Like this person
7
6 - Somewhat like this person
5 - Somewhat unlike this person
4
3 - Unlike this person
2
1 - Definitely unlike this person

Item	Raters	Average	1 2 3 4 5 6 7 8 9 10
1. Motivates others effectively.	14	7.6	A
7. Gives others recognition for their accomplishments.	14	7.7	A
9. Helps others to see the importance of their work.	14	7.6	A
12. Involves people in decisions that affect them.	14	6.9	A
21. Encourages new ideas and procedures.	14	7.4	A
25. Allows subordinates to make decisions when appropriate.	14	7.9	A
27. Uses subordinate suggestions well.	14	7.2	A
28. Gives subordinates the authority to do their work.	13	8.1	A
Empowerment		7.5	A

Item	Raters	Average	1 2 3 4 5 6 7 8 9 10
4. Shows consideration for others.	14	7.6	A
15. Is receptive to feedback.	14	6.5	A
20. Shows sensitivity to others' feelings.	14	8.4	A
22. Expresses feelings openly.	14	7.5	A
23. Listens to others effectively.	13	8.5	A
24. Has a good sense of humor.	13	7.8	A
29. Counsels with subordinates on their personal concerns.	14	9.3	A
Interpersonal		7.9	A

Item	Raters	Average	1 2 3 4 5 6 7 8 9 10
14. Helps others to develop their abilities.	13	8.5	A
19. Coaches others in developing their skills.	14	7.4	A
Development		8.0	A

Index Summary for Pat Armstrong

Item	Raters	Average	1 2 3 4 5 6 7 8 9 10
3. Gives others constructive criticism.	14	8.8	
8. Lets others know how well they are doing.	14	7.5	
11. Confronts others in a skillful manner.	14	7.4	
17. Adapts his/her leadership style to individuals.	14	7.3	
18. Communicates well with others.	14	7.2	
Feedback		7.6	A

Item	Raters	Average	1 2 3 4 5 6 7 8 9 10
2. Explains new tasks clearly.	14	7.3	
5. Works well with others in setting their goals.	14	7.2	
6. Establishes clear job-task expectations.	14	7.7	
10. Delegates tasks appropriately.	14	7.9	
16. Organizes projects effectively.	14	6.7	
26. Keeps job roles clear.	14	8.4	
30. Provides appropriate resources for subordinates.	14	7.0	
Task Skills		7.5	A

Item	Raters	Average	1 2 3 4 5 6 7 8 9 10
13. Evaluates the performance of others effectively.	14	7.2	
31. Monitors the task performance of subordinates.	14	9.6	
32. Maintains performance standards.	13	8.5	
Performance		8.4	A

Summary for All Indexes

Item	Average	1 2 3 4 5 6 7 8 9 10
Empowerment	7.5	
XYZCO	8.4	
Interpersonal	7.9	
XYZCO	8.6	
Development	8.0	
XYZCO	8.5	
Feedback	7.6	
XYZCO	8.4	
Task Skills	7.5	
XYZCO	8.5	
Performance	8.4	
XYZCO	8.7	
Armstrong	7.7	
XYZCO	8.5	

Considerations in Developing Reports

We strongly recommend that you consider the following criteria when developing the statistical summaries of 360° feedback reports.

- **Level of detail.** Keep the feedback reports as simple and uncomplicated as possible. Work toward making it likely that the feedback recipient can accurately interpret the reports in the absence of a professional facilitator or consultant, even months after the individual receives the information.

- **Probable receptivity.** It is critical that the targeted individuals respond to the 360° feedback in an open manner. That means that there should be no implied judgment in the feedback reports and that the display of the data is not shocking or threatening in any way. Since color printing is becoming widely available, it is tempting to color-code "desirable" and "undesirable" ratings. We recommend that all evaluation, expressed or implied, be the responsibility of the feedback recipient. It is important that 360° feedback not be experienced as a "report card." It is equally important to cast the feedback into a form that is understandable to people who may not be comfortable with numbers, particularly statistics.

- **Time for feedback work.** Since feeding back the statistics is only the first step in the growth-producing processes of self-confrontation and action planning, it is important not to provide more information or complex reports that cannot be adequately used by recipients in the planned feedback session. If you have budgeted only one hour for the feedback experience, restrict the level and depth of reports severely.

- **Links to planning.** Using 360° assessment data to inform individuals of how they are perceived is not an exercise in "gotcha." It is more properly a service that gives individuals needed data on which they can construct self-directed action plans for personal and professional improvement. All of the content of the questionnaire, the feedback reports, and other information made available during the feedback session should have clear links to this planning. We discuss how to design and conduct these sessions in the next chapter.

The Final Feedback Package

The 360° feedback package for one recipient should be sealed, and no one should be able to see it except the person who prints the reports. Inside there should be a document that recaps the entire 360° feedback intervention. The package should include a blank copy of the questionnaire that was used to gather the ratings. Next should come a short series of feedback reports. Each of these reports should be preceded by a simple sheet of directions regarding how to interpret the data and followed by one or more action-planning worksheets, such as those in Appendix B.

Feedback recipients have the right to expect that their data will be secure at all times, that no one will see their feedback packages except if they choose to show them themselves, and that what they receive will be understandable and useful.

Chapter 16

360° Feedback and
Action Planning

The overarching goal of 360° feedback is to inform and motivate feedback recipients to engage in self-directed action planning for improvement. It is the feedback process, not the measurement process, that generates the real payoffs. In this chapter, we focus on strategies for maximizing those payoffs. First we discuss how to interpret 360° feedback reports and construct action-planning guides; then we turn our attention to working one-on-one with feedback recipients, present a step-by-step procedure for working with recipient groups, and explain how to combine the one-on-one and group methods.

Interpreting 360° Feedback Reports

It is important to bear in mind that 360° feedback packages are usually the confidential property of their recipients. Unless your intervention has special conditions that everyone understands before participation begins, you need to honor the privacy of these data. We strongly recommend that 360° feedback reports be sealed, then opened by the feedback recipient. Remember, since such data are often threatening, it is vital that the recipient trust the confidentiality of process that generated the information.

Basic Principles

Here are four fundamental principles to consider as you contemplate and prepare for providing 360° feedback:

- **The locus of evaluation is the feedback recipient.** Your interpretation and evaluation are irrelevant. As a feedback and action-planning facilitator, your job is not to show the person what the numbers mean. Many 360° feedback recipients experience their data as a "report card." It is important to help feedback recipients put their own meaning into the reports and reach their own conclusions regarding "how well they came out."

- **Whatever is perceived is real.** A friend of ours puts it this way: "Whatever appears to be is *always* more significant than what is." What the 360° feedback recipient sees in his or her reports *is* real for that person at that time. Your job is to ensure that the recipient is adequately informed in the process.

- **Avoid the "paralysis of analysis."** Technical and scientific people tend to focus more on the statistics than on the quality of human relationships and competencies needed to be effective within the organization. A feedback recipient who concentrates on the technicalities of the measurement and feedback needs your help in order to go beyond those concerns to "So what?" and "What now?"

- **Combat data denial.** We have often remarked that humans are the only animals capable of self-deception. Most of us tend to be good at it, and well equipped to go on the defensive should anyone threaten our comfortable notions about ourselves. It is therefore not surprising that, when faced with 360° feedback data, many recipients feel threatened and react self-defensively, arguing over the data or blaming others for the assessment results. In such a situation, concentrate on getting the recipient to see the effects of the differences between the self-assessment and the "other" assessments, and to confront the possibility that a conflicting view may be valid.

Feeding back 360° assessment information is a touchy process. It requires skill, courage, and structure. It also requires that the facilitator be knowledgeable about simple, descriptive statistics.

Basic Statistics

There are two basic types of statistics, descriptive and inferential. *Descriptive* statistics summarize a set of data in straightforward terms. *Inferential* statistics tell whether a sample taken from a large group (people or things) supports conclusions about that group. For example, if you took a sample of balls from a closed container that included lots of them, you might be able, through inferential statistics, to conclude that in the container there is a certain percentage of red balls. In practice, almost all 360° feedback statistics are descriptive. This makes the feedback process easier, since we do not have to deal with estimates of chance. In general, we avoid discussions of "significant differences" and probability levels in 360° feedback.

Here are the most common statistics that appear in 360° feedback reports:

- **Frequency/Number/Percent.** Frequency is the number of people who rated the recipient the same way on a given assessment-questionnaire item. Converting that value to a percentage requires dividing it by the total number of people who rated the recipient.

- **Cumulative frequency/Number/Percent.** Cumulative frequency refers to the number of people who rated the individual on a given item at a given rating *or lower*. Converting that number to a percentage requires dividing it by the total number of persons who rated the individual. For example, consider the following set of ratings for one item.

To what degree does this person show competence in finding innovative ways to meet customer needs?

Scale	Freq.	%	Cum. Freq.	Cum. %
To a very great degree	2	14	14	100
To a great degree	2	14	12	85
To some degree	3	21	10	71
To a small degree	4	29	7	50
To a very small degree	2	14	3	21
Not at all	1	7	1	7

Two people rated this recipient "To a very great degree." That represents 14% of his or her panel of raters. Half of the raters indicated that the recipient shows this competency to a small degree or less.

- **Range.** This is simply the highest and lowest ratings a person receives on a given item. In the above example, the range is 6 points, or 1 to 6.

- **Average/Norm.** This is one of the most common 360° feedback statistics, and it can be one of the most misleading. The average is simply the sum of the recipient's score on an item, or set of items, divided by the number of ratings. To calculate the average score on the sample item above, we would add the rating points and divide by 14. The *mean* is the same as this arithmetic average, 3.6 in the case of the sample.

- **Weighted average.** Sometimes organizations apply different weights to the sources of data in 360° assessments. For example, they might assign a weight of 0.5 to self-ratings, 1.0 to boss ratings, 0.75 to peer ratings, and 1.0 to subordinate ratings. The average, or mean, then comes from multiplying each rating by its assigned weight before adding the points and dividing by the number of ratings. This practice can be confusing to feedback recipients; it is almost always done for the benefit of the organization rather than for the benefit of providing developmental feedback. As a result, we rarely recommend its use.

- **Standard deviation.** Technically, this is the root mean squared deviation from the mean. In simpler terms, it is an index of the degree to which a person's ratings are dispersed, or spread out. The larger the standard deviation, the more a feedback recipient's ratings vary on an item or set of items. Since few feedback recipients understand this statistic, it is ordinarily omitted from 360° feedback reports.

Effective Practices

Presenting 360° feedback reports requires careful study and preparation. The first step is, of course, to become thoroughly familiar with the format of the reports yourself. This means studying a sample report so that you can feel sufficiently comfortable working with individuals and groups of feedback recipients on such information. Anticipate questions that they may ask, and watch for any signs of confusion or apprehension. Rehearse ways to guide them through the feedback without doing the tasks of interpreting and planning for them.

Present 360° feedback reports positively, without implied threats. If you have gone through the process yourself, as we recommend, "sell" feedback recipients on the benefits of taking the data seriously and working through it systematically; then leave feedback recipients to draw their own conclusions. Emphasize the need to begin developing self-directed action plans immediately.

There are several things to avoid when presenting 360° feedback. First, avoid drawing your own conclusions from anyone's data or adding your judgments to the reports. As we have stressed, avoid interpreting the feedback for recipients. Finally, strenuously avoid selling your own solutions. Individuals need to develop their improvement plans on their own terms. Your job is to act as a resource for them during the process. By facing the information honestly and deciding themselves what to do about it, recipients are more likely to develop a solid commitment to their action plans.

During data analysis there is a tendency for feedback recipients to discount their strengths and to focus on their "warts" instead. It is important to get individuals to acknowledge and take personal credit for their developed competencies. The feedback process should turn weaknesses into opportunities for improvement. Feedback recipients need to learn that all perceptions are valid and important. And they need to develop discipline in analyzing themselves.

During the diagnostic phase of the feedback process, initially encourage recipients to focus on their strengths; then ask them to compare their self-perceptions to their raters' perceptions of them. Move on to identifying opportunities for improvement. Challenge recipients to identify their lowest-rated items and to give those items careful consideration.

The planning phase comes next. This often entails helping recipients overcome self-defensiveness and accept the need for improvement. Guide them into setting measurable objectives and planning for the support of others. Note the SPIRO criteria for effective plans in Appendix B, and use this model to help them test their intentions. It is also good practice to provide a list of organizational and community resources for feedback recipients to consider during their planning for self-improvement. This list may include training, academic programs, counseling assistance, and other similar resources, including contract information.

In follow-through, offer to conduct the survey again for individuals who want to pursue the process further. Also offer to facilitate team building with recipients' work groups when that is an appropriate intervention. If an individual is in a conflict situation with others, offer to function as a third-party facilitator for them. Plan check-up meetings with individual recipients and 360° feedback groups.

Remember: It is important to prevent 360° feedback from being taken lightly. Help feedback recipients set themselves up for successes. Offer to consult during the implementation of their plans.

Action-Planning Guides

Action-planning guides are worksheets that lead the recipient through feedback analysis and action-plan development (see Appendix B for examples). They accompany the data reports in the feedback package, and their contents closely parallel the information in the reports. The feedback recipient ends up with a comprehensive plan for self-improvement, including closing perception gaps between self and others.

Developing Action-Planning Guides: Major Considerations

There are two important things to keep in mind when developing action-planning guides:

- The purpose of the 360° assessment
- The recipient's commitment to the implementation of his or her action plan.

Purpose. The worksheets must focus on the reasons for the assessment, with the data analysis structured so that recipients can easily make sense out of their data, even in the absence of a facilitator.

Commitment. The worksheets, as well as the entire process of feeding back 360° assessment data, must serve the goal of developing and solidifying the recipient's commitment to self-improvement. The individual should come away from the experience ready and willing to do whatever it takes to implement his or her action plan. This means that the construction of the worksheets should be based on some model that facilitates the development of commitment.

In addition to the above, remember that action-planning guides should ensure thoroughness in analysis and planning. Presenting the steps of analysis and planning in sequence on the worksheets will help in that regard. As these worksheets must facilitate the development of concrete plans for self-improvement, tie the feedback process to effective processes for self-discovery and commitment. Also, develop "real-time" learning about planning and process as well as about the self.

One-on-One 360° Feedback Delivery

This is a viable form of feedback delivery. Timmreck (1995) gives us further survey findings on the large consortium whose member organizations routinely use

360° assessment (see Chapter 1). These findings indicate that, at the time of the survey, about one in six used one-on-one consultation (45% simply mailed the reports to recipients, and about 23% fed them back in workshops).

Three objectives guide the practice of providing 360° feedback one-on-one to individuals:

- Guaranteeing thoroughness in analysis
- Ensuring that recipients understand the options available to them
- Gaining the recipients' commitment to the implementation of their action plans

Recipients will most likely make wise planning decisions if they (1) understand how others perceive them, (2) know what help is available for self-improvement, and (3) are willing to take personal responsibility for what they decide to do about their own development.

Providing 360° feedback and facilitating action planning is somewhat like counseling in that the process is essentially permissive, nonjudgmental, and nonmanipulative. It is almost always also confidential, but, as Dalton (1995) points out, "there has been a move toward making the feedback public, at least to the manager's boss" (p. 3). Your job in any one-on-one consultation is to be resourceful and to focus in a client-centered way on the recipient's goals and intentions. It is important to remember, however, that permissiveness does not mean passivity; you must be an *active resource* for the person.

The Group Session

One-on-one 360° feedback delivery is facilitator-intensive. Presenting such information in group settings can be easier on the facilitator, as well as more economical. Designing and facilitating a 360° feedback session for a group of recipients requires careful consideration, however.

Here is a useful design for group sessions that equips you with a step-by-step procedure for maximizing the beneficial impact of the feedback. Each step has been thoroughly tested and the steps carefully sequenced. The design helps participants make sense out of their feedback, and they walk away with a clear commitment to a self-directed action plan for skills improvement and career development. This procedure assumes that you will provide a strengths/needs report, a force-field worksheet, a gap report, and worksheets on strengths and needs. You will also need to be familiar with the SPIRO model that is included in Appendix B.

1. **Preparing for the session.** Study this design before each feedback session. Review the session's objectives with the senior leader(s) who are assisting you. Make copies of the handouts you will need, and arrange them in the order that you will use them. Remind yourself that receiving feedback makes most people anxious, that this is the first feedback session for most partici-pants, and that you are in their service. Have the meeting room arranged so that people can work privately as well as hold discussions with you. There are no audiovisual requirements for the session, but you may want to have a flipchart and markers available. Also, you may wish to make overheads of selected pages of a sample report and use them for illustrating how to read the ratings. You may wish to make posters of the session's opening topics— goals, roles, getting value, and session overview—outlined below.

2. **Greeting participants.** Get there early, and personally greet each participant. Attempt to put them at ease, and keep your demeanor positive.

3. **Opening the session.** Usually the senior leader opens the session, formally introduces you, and then presents the following:

   - *Goals:* (1) To understand the 360° feedback; (2) to develop self-directed action plans for skills improvement and career development.

   - *Roles:* Facilitators will guide the feedback analysis and planning; participants will study their personal statistical results and turn them into plans they are committed to carrying out.

   - *Getting Value:* (1) Take the feedback as information; (2) plan for needed clarification; (3) take personal responsibility; (4) commit yourself to following through on your plans.

   - *Session Overview:* After a brief discussion of the 360° feedback, parti-cipants will study their personal feedback packages and develop self-directed action plans. The session will last no more than three hours, and it is important that everyone remain in attendance throughout.

4. **Preparing for feedback.** This is a brief lecturette on the subject of the 360° feedback, how it differs from performance review, and some cautions for participants to take when they receive their feedback packages.

5. **Distributing the feedback packages.** Just before you pass out the packages, explain the contents of the Isolating Strengths worksheet. Participants will then use the Strengths and Needs report (in their packages) to complete the worksheet.

6. **Areas for improvement.** Participants use the same statistical report to isolate the areas of most needed improvement in their present, and any career-advancing, jobs.

7. **Force-field analysis.** Before they rush to conclusions about their areas of needed improvement, introduce a useful tool for analyzing the skills that they need to develop. Participants should use it to work through two or three areas.

8. **SPIRO lecturette.** Before they commit themselves to an action plan, explain the five criteria of effective planning.

9. **Support resources.** Another part of planning is looking at what we can use to support our development. Participants work through an analysis of what is available to them both interpersonally and in terms of developmental opportunities.

10. **The Gap Report.** This part of the 360° feedback shows participants the largest differences between their self-ratings and those of others. They work through an analysis of this feedback report and plan actions to close these perception gaps after the session.

11. **Following through.** In this section of the feedback session, participants plan two types of meetings: one with their bosses, and one with their other feedback providers. They study step-by-step methods for following through with the people who supplied their feedback.

12. **Gantt charting.** In this section of the design, participants make an action schedule that becomes their completed Self-Directed Action Timeline. This is not a career timeline; it is a planning chart of the steps they will take to follow through on their feedback.

13. **Measures.** The old saying is, "What gets measured gets done." This part of the feedback session focuses on establishing definite measurement strategies for mapping progress on their action plans.

14. **Supporting others.** Since people in an organization are interdependent, it is important that they understand it is in their own selfish interest to lend support to one another as they develop. This is a brief discussion that attempts to elicit supportive behavior from participants in the future.

15. **Committing.** The final part of the 360° feedback session is about "putting yourself on the line." Participants write out a commitment statement and turn in a copy, to be mailed back to them later. The facilitator(s) close the session in a positive manner.

A Combined Strategy

Some organizations provide 360° feedback in group sessions, followed by private, individual "coaching sessions." During the group meetings the facilitator goes over the purposes of the intervention, demonstrates how to read the feedback reports, and schedules an appointment with each individual, usually beginning immediately. The rationale for this approach is that the group sessions shorten the time required for coaching and engender a kind of peer pressure to take the process seriously. This strategy requires that you prepare a sample feedback report and display it (usually on overhead transparencies). You test the feedback recipient's ability to interpret the data and understand the planning process. The individual sessions that immediately follow the group meetings are private and confidential.

Follow-Through

It is essential that 360° feedback not be a one-time event. This means that any use of this technology must include a follow-through whereby feedback recipients provide coaching and counseling as well as reinforcement of progress in skill development. Huzucha, Hezlett, and Schneider (1993) found that regularly reviewing plans and progress maintains the momentum of 360° feedback. They point out that the feedback recipient's supervisor should play an active role in follow-through, not just "provide support." They need to be ready, willing, and able to provide timely, specific suggestions for further progress.

If you deliver 360° feedback one-on-one, you can contract with each feedback recipient regarding your role in following through on the person's self-directed action plan. When you deliver the feedback reports in group settings, you can signal your availability to work with any or all of the individuals throughout the period until their 360° reassessment.

Chapter 17

Longitudinal Assessment

Using 360° assessments to track the growth of individuals and groups over time requires special considerations. This chapter lays out the usual practices, as well as some of the psychological repercussions of feeding back repeat data, and briefly discusses the difficulty in measuring change in individuals and organizations.

Repeat Surveys

The most common practice in the use of 360° feedback is to make the feedback intervention a "one-shot deal"; that is, feedback recipients get data only once, or on questionnaires that cannot be compared to one another. Most organizations are not now giving their employees *any* multirater feedback, and few are using repeat surveys to provide feedback across time. Even fewer are using 360° assessments to track the payoffs of their training and developmental effects.

When organizations do use repeat surveys with exactly the same measurement instruments, they can offer hard, objective evidence to individuals about the outcomes of their self-improvement programs. Also, when group trends among the recipients of 360° feedback are analyzed, it is possible to discover not only the recipient's common developmental needs but also areas in which they are developing the competencies that the organization needs in place among its people. Approaching training-needs and outcomes assessments in this way sharply targets your training programs and models accountability in the HRD function as well. While the primary motivation for conducting repeat 360° surveys should, in our view, be to provide reliable, valid information to individuals regarding how they are perceived by self and others, the secondary benefits of this practice can be significant.

"Then-and-Now" Comparisons for Individuals

It is important to be mindful of how feedback on repeated surveys can threaten feedback recipients. They may consider the feedback a "report card" on progress or a set of results on their efforts toward personal and professional improvement. To combat these misperceptions, it is imperative that the principles discussed in the previous chapter guide the feedback process.

Some feedback recipients, looking at their comparative statistics, may ask, "How much difference does it take to be significant?" The answer to the question is, of course, "It depends." What it depends on are such factors as the length of the rating scale, the number and dispersion of ratings, the reliability of the measurement, and the conditions under which the two surveys were taken. The question is legitimate, but the answer is a bit slippery. What you need to avoid is an unnecessarily technical response or oversimplifications. The feedback recipient should focus on the overall *trends* in his or her data, not on the absolute differences between ratings and averages. It is tempting to give a rule of thumb, such as two points between individual raters or a half-point between two averages, but this practice can be both inaccurate and misleading. Get them to move beyond the question and into the analysis of trends.

Studying Groups of Participants across Time

One by-product of repeated 360° degree assessments is the ability to track growth in groups of people across time. This can be a central part of assessing the payoffs of developmental programs in the organization.

If, for example, you are instituting a new supervisory-skills training program, you may want to use a 360° survey to choose the appropriate modules, based on the lowest average competencies. You would, of course, provide feedback to the individuals on which the assessment was taken, but one of your purposes would be to analyze the group statistics in order to prioritize the training content.

After a significant number of supervisors have gone through the training experience, you would repeat the 360° assessment on them, in order to study changes in the targeted competencies. You would give "then-now" feedback to these individuals, and you would analyze their group's trends for evidence of how effective the training has been.

Traps in Measuring Change

Determining the extent to which individuals and groups of 360° feedback recipients change over time is not a simple matter. In our companion book, *Surveying Employees* (Jones & Bearley, 1995b), we point out the following:

> Consider, for instance, the concern about "instrument reactivity" (Spector, 1981). Completing a survey questionnaire has an effect on the employee. So the act of measuring changes the thing being measured. Harris (1963) specified the vagaries of mapping change in great detail.
>
> Innumerable events can influence changes in organizational functioning and work life between surveys, of course. The comparative data need to be interpreted carefully, and the trap of oversimplifying needs to be avoided assiduously. The fact that an index went up or down may be due to any number of occurrences. The item may even be interpreted differently at different times. Chubb (1987) termed this phenomenon "temporal validity."

Keep a record of significant changes that the organization undergoes during the period between the two assessments. This can be invaluable in interpreting change statistics.

Sometimes 360° feedback recipients can become complacent regarding their repeated data. It is important in providing longitudinal 360° feedback for them to be able both to celebrate their growth and to make new self-directed plans for personal and professional development. Ideally, the process never stops.

Chapter 18

Reliability, Validity, and Norms in 360° Feedback

Facilitators of 360° feedback need to be aware of the technical characteristics and limitations of the data involved. This chapter briefly discusses why these concerns are important, defines some technical terminology, spells out our point of view, and describes common research methods for investigating reliability.

Why Technical Considerations Are Important

Paying attention to technical matters in 360° feedback is far less exciting than "seeing the lights go on" as feedback recipients study their data and make improvement plans. But we must be cognizant of the limitations of the data sets on which our feedback reports are constructed. People who approve 360° feedback interventions sometimes ask about reliability, validity, and the availability of "industry norms." Feedback recipients sometimes ask about similar concerns. Human resource professionals need some insight into the precision and coverage of our 360° assessments. Finally, the total quality movement has focused many people's attention on standards and benchmarks.

Definitions

Here are basic definitions of the three terms most commonly used to denote the technicalities of 360° assessments.

- **Reliability:** A measure of stability, repeatability, consistency, or comparability. In assessment terms, reliability is usually a question of how much confidence can be placed in the accuracy of the ratings. The usual methods of exploring the reliability of a 360° assessment questionnaire include *"test-retest"* (comparing ratings for the same individuals over a relatively short time), *alternate forms* (using parallel forms of the assessment instrument to determine the extent to which the same patterns of ratings emerge), *internal consistency* (usually Chronbach's alpha statistic), and *intraclass* (comparing the amount of agreement among multiple judges or raters). These comparisons are almost always in the form of correlation coefficients, ranging from 0.00 (no reliability) to 1.00 (perfect reliability).

- **Validity:** A measure of the usefulness of a procedure, technique, or device. Its most common aspects are *"face"* (how credible is the assessment on the part of your raters), *content* (the extent to which the assessment covers the subject comprehensively), *correlative* (the degree to which the instrument agrees with older, more established measures of the same thing), *criterion-referenced* (the ability to predict future performance from data off the instrument), and *construct* (what the instrument actually measures). It is not possible to answer the question "Is this questionnaire valid?" You would have to know, "For what purpose?"

- **Norms:** Descriptive statistics on a "population," a sample, or a known group. Usually these are expressed in terms of averages or percentiles. It is important to remember that statistical norms are not standards. They are "what is" rather than "what should be." Most important, they must be meaningful to 360° feedback recipients. Norms may be *internal* (you derive them from the ratings you collect) or *external* ("industry," or statistical comparisons with groups outside the organization).

The Study of Reliability, Validity, and Norms

Reliability, validity, and norms need to be studied locally. Off-the-shelf 360° assessment instruments, while appearing to be well constructed technically and presented attractively, may have little or no usefulness locally. Our strong position is that no assessment instrument is either valid or invalid. It depends on the particular use of the instrument by a particular professional in a particular organizational context. Validity is *always* situation-specific; it does not reside in the questionnaire or its items.

Reliability and validity in 360° feedback instruments depend on the methods used for constructing the questionnaire, the rating scale, the content of the items, the climate of the organization, the reliability and validity of criterion measures, and probably many other factors. That is why we recommend that you develop your own 360° assessment questionnaires if you want them to have high content and face validity.

Norms can be both informative and highly misleading to 360° feedback recipients. We strongly favor your developing your own norms within the organization rather than relying on industry or national norms. This is the same argument we make for all employee and customer surveys as well (Jones & Bearley, 1995b). Locally derived norms are superior to outside ones because they are completely understandable to feedback recipients. Your people know the conditions under which the data were collected, and they are familiar with the people with whom they are being compared. In the case of outside norms, you never quite know how representative the people were who were assessed, how effective they were, the conditions under which their assessments were carried out, and the like. Developing your own norms means that your can build your own 360° assessment instruments to be completely valid in content. Often the standardized ones do not cover precisely your client organizations' priorities, competency models, and values. The usefulness of normative-comparison data is greatly enhanced when you build your own norms and use them in your 360° feedback processes.

Research Methods

You do not have to be a statistician in order to conduct your own studies of reliability, validity, and norms in 360° feedback, although it helps if you have access to one. Here are some ways of exploring these technical concerns within your client organizations.

Sample retests. You assess a group of individuals, as rated by self and others. After 2 to 4 weeks, you collect their ratings again, with no feedback after the first round. Then you analyze the extent to which the same ratings and patterns occurred the second time, compared to the first. You have to allow enough time between assessments so that people will not remember their exact ratings and simply repeat them from memory; however, too long a period can mean that individuals change their perceptions during the interim.

Internal consistency analysis. There is a trap in thinking that the raters must agree on their perceptions of an individual in order for their data to be reliable. There may be honest, stable, real differences in perceptions, based on different observational sets of the raters. We do not recommend, then, that you consider intraclass correlation to be useful in determining the consistency of ratings. We use the Chronbach alpha statistic to analyze the ratings of groups of participants. This analysis is particularly useful in studying how items in "indexes," or sets of 360° assessment questionnaire items, hang together.

Factor analysis. One way to explore the dimensions within your 360° assessment questionnaire is to subject the ratings to some sort of factor-analytical procedure. We use principle-components analysis in order to study the intercorrelations among questionnaire items. These studies are highly technical, and we recommend that you consult an appropriate statistician for assistance in carrying them out and interpreting the results. Factor analysis is a good empirical way of establishing clusters of items to become indexes for use in 360° feedback.

Multiple regression analysis. This type of study involves establishing a success criterion and then correlating data from your 360° assessment with it, using your entire data set all at once. The procedure identifies the particular set of questionnaire items or indexes that, taken together, have the most productive validity regarding the criterion. The most difficult problem with such studies is specifying and measuring the criterion. Everyone knows, for example, that performance-review ratings are largely worthless statistically, so avoid using them as your criterion. Look for ways of measuring such things as productivity, profitability, loyalty, teamwork, and creativity and innovation.

Discriminant analysis. This statistical procedure compares two or more groups of people against their 360° assessment profiles. You might consider a group from one organizational level versus a group from another organizational level, high-potential individuals versus others at their level, or people who have gone through your training versus others like them who have not received the training. The analyses isolate those questionnaire items (and their relative importance) that account for differences among the groups you study.

Contrasts of organizational units. If one part of the organization goes through 360° feedback and another, comparable one does not, you can study their overall effectiveness as evidence of the efficacy of your intervention. You may also analyze your overall 360° assessment data by organizational unit. Your conclusions should not be surprises.

Tracking action plans. Since the major goal of 360° feedback interventions is for individuals to commit themselves to implementing well-constructed action plans for personal and professional improvement, you may choose to follow up feedback recipients to see whether they are actually doing what they committed to do. If your feedback process works well, they will still be working toward the goals they set during the feedback sessions, will have achieved some (at least partially), and will have gone on to other priorities. You can consider using personal interviews, group sessions, and anonymous surveys to gather data on their progress and achievements. You may also want to solicit comparable data from people other than the feedback recipients themselves.

Surveys of 360° feedback effectiveness. One easy-to-conduct study involves surveying feedback recipients (and perhaps their managers, subordinates, and/or co-workers) regarding how effectively the intervention has promoted their taking responsibility for, and achieving, personal and professional growth as a result of your intervention. This should be a "quick and dirty" survey that focuses solely on how much the individual has grown and how helpful his or her feedback and action planning have been.

Answering Questions about Validity

How do you answer the person who asks, "Is this questionnaire valid?" As we pointed out earlier, you need to ground your response in purpose. Here are some defensible answers, depending on the context of your 360° feedback intervention.

- The instrument covers the competencies (e.g., traits, skills, knowledge) that the organization deems important for its people to develop. It has clear content validity.

- The questionnaire contains only items that meet established validity criteria regarding clear, unidimensional, unambiguous, ratable content (see Chapter 14).

- Feedback recipients have found that the feedback from this instrument is believable and useful to them in their action planning for self-improvement.

Human resource professionals tend to dread having to answer technical questions about 360° assessment instruments. Such questions are often anticipated from personnel who have scientific and technical backgrounds. It is important to respond factually and nondefensively. The questions may be genuine requests for information, which you need to be prepared to provide.

Chapter 19

Getting Started in 360° Feedback

You may be saying to yourself, " This 360° feedback intervention stuff is hard to pull off." And you may be right—for your client organization. In this chapter we outline some strategies for you to consider in launching the use of 360° feedback technology.

Easy-to-Sell Options

Here are some uses of 360° feedback that are easier to sell and implement than wholesale interventions that can involve hundred or thousands of raters.

- **One-on-one consultations** with individual leaders. Often you can establish sufficient rapport with one or more highly situated organizational leaders that you can sell them on the idea of conducting 360° assessments on themselves. Then you can implement a plan such as the following:

  1. Adapt the *Survey of Needed Competencies* (Appendix C) to your situation. Develop a customized assessment instrument for the particular leader, getting his or her buy-in for the content, scale, and format.
  2. Conduct the survey with the leader.
  3. Analyze the data and prepare a confidential feedback report.
  4. Work through the data and planning with the leader.
  5. Assist the leader in following through on his or her self-directed action plans.

- **Needs assessment for a new management-development course.** Use 360° assessment on potential course participants instead of the traditional anonymous needs-assessment survey. Use a plan such as the following:

1. Analyze your course-design options. Consider time, timing, number of participants, venue, cost, and other factors.
2. Identify "target" leaders. For whom is the course to be developed?
3. Solicit their cooperation with peer- and subordinate-feedback assessments of them, along with their self-ratings.
4. Conduct the survey and prepare individual feedback reports.
5. Draft the course design to cover what you identify as common opportunities for improvement.
6. Deliver the reports and the design draft to the prospective attendees.
7. Redesign according to their feedback on your draft.
8. Schedule the course.
9. Recruit participants.

- **Survey on yourself.** This is a completely customized assessment of both your competencies and the effectiveness of the services you perform. Use a sequence of steps such as these:

1. Develop a list of needed competencies and services performed in your position.
2. Identify data sources, people who are qualified to rate you.
3. Solicit feedback through a survey.
4. Complete self-assessment, including making your own predictions of feedback trends.
5. Analyze gaps and plan improvements.
6. Follow through with your feedback panel.

Working with the Executive Team

If you have access to the senior-leadership team, you could develop a simple self-and-other assessment to use with them anonymously, perhaps within a team-building session. They could then discuss how doing a more thorough assessment of all organizational leaders can benefit both those individuals and the organization.

You can be assertive in communicating the leadership-development implications of the organization's purpose/mission/vision statements. Often these provide the most appropriate content for developing the organization's competency model. They help to give your 360° assessment questionnaire high, and obvious, content validity. Take each of the organization's values, for example, and ask, "What competencies (skills, knowledge, traits) do our people need to have in order to live out this value most effectively?" You will usually find that each value takes several questionnaire items to measure adequately.

Alternatively, you can engage the senior-executive team in specifying the needed competencies by using the *Survey of Needed Competencies* in Appendix C. This questionnaire can be given to the team, and the results reviewed with them, or it can be used in the following way. First, conduct an anonymous survey of the team's subordinates (the *Survey* is a particularly good instrument for such polling); next, bring the survey results to a work session with the team and solicit their opinions before publishing the results; finally, help the team complete the *Data-Source Worksheet* (in Appendix D) to determine who will participate as a rater in the 360° assessment and (optionally) how much weight their data will be assigned. Many senior-executive teams prefer to weight all data sources equally.

The available research on the outcomes of training interventions strongly indicates that what happens before and after the training contributes most to its effectiveness (Broad & Newstrom, 1992). What trainers actually do while facilitating courses rapidly dissipates unless there is adequate, active support of trainees before and after attendance. Simply including 360° feedback in courses may not be enough. You may have to find ways of enrolling senior managers and supervisors in taking the problem of training transfer seriously. Essential among the possibilities is getting the leaders' commitment to model effective follow-through and to apply course learning to everyday job situations, and then coaching the leaders in this task. Obtaining their commitment will be easier if you enlist their help by their making presentations in training courses. You should provide them with a sensible context for their participation and help them become oriented to that context; then, as you assist them during the 360° feedback process, you can urge them to model an acceptance of the process (including assessment results and feedback) and a determination to follow-through on their self-directed action plans later.

A Concluding Note

This technology is developing rapidly as more organizations see the value of providing solid information to their people about how they are perceived. Some people are experimenting with electronic forms of data collection and feedback. Others are attempting to integrate 360° assessment methods with performance review, succession planning, and career planning. We are confident that these developments are not a fad. We believe that the use of multirater feedback will become a staple intervention within medium- to large-sized organizations. If you have not yet started to use this technology, we hope that this book has inspired you to begin testing it in your client organizations.

References

Barclay, J. H., & Harland, L. K. (1995, March). *Peer performance appraisals. Group and Organizational Management, 20* (1), 39-60.

Bennis, W. B., & Nanus, B. (1985). *Leaders: Strategies for taking charge.* New York: Harper & Row.

Bernardin, J., & Hagan, C. (1995, May). *The effects of a 360-degree appraisal system on managerial performance: No matter how cynical I get, I can't keep up.* Paper presented at the Annual Conference of the Society for Industrial and Organizational Psychology, Orlando, FL.

Bigelow, J. D. (1991). *Managerial skills: Explorations in practical knowledge.* Newbury Park, CA: Sage.

Bracken, D. W. (1994, September). Straight talk about multirater feedback. *Training and Development*, 44-51.

Bratton, D. A. (1994, November). *Enhancing corporate success: Linking salary and incentives to the achievement of results.* Paper presented to the Institute for International Research Conference on Performance Appraisal, Toronto, Canada.

Broad, M. L., & Newstrom, J. W. (1992). *Transfer of training.* Reading, MA: Addison-Wesley.

Byham, W. C., & Associates. (1987). *Dimensions of effective performance for the 1990s: What they are, how they differ among levels, how they are changing.* Pittsburgh, PA: Development Dimensions International.

Campbell, J. P., Campbell, R. J., & Associates (1988). *Productivity in organizations.* San Francisco, CA: Jossey-Bass.

Carew, J. (1989, March). When salespeople evaluate their managers. *Sales & Marketing Management*, 24-26.

Carey, R. (1995, March). Coming around to 360-degree feedback. *Incentive,* 55-60.

Chubb, J. E. (1987). Multiple indicators and measurement error in panel data: An evaluation of summated scales, path analysis, and confirmatory maximum likelihood factor analysis. *Political Methodology, 5,* 413-444.

Clark, K. E., & Clark, M. B. (Eds.). (1990). *Measures of leadership.* Greensboro, NC: Center for Creative Leadership.

Dalton, M. (1995, May). *Multirater feedback and conditions for change.* Presentation at the Annual Conference of the Society for Industrial and Organizational Psychology, Orlando, FL.

Daniels, A. (1989). *Performance management.* Tucker, GA: Performance Management Publications.

Del Balzo, J. M., & Miller, A. (1989, March). A new organizational flight pattern. *Training and Development Journal,* 41-42.

Denton, W. E. (1994, May-June). Developing employee skills to match company needs. *Credit World*, *82* (5), 19-20.

Edwards, M. (1994). Minimizing time investment. *Perspectives.* Tempe, AZ: TEAMS.

Egan, G. (1994). *Working the shadow side: A guide to positive behind-the-scenes management.* San Francisco, CA: Jossey-Bass.

Harris, W. W. (Ed.). (1963). *Problems in measuring change.* Madison, WI: University of Wisconsin Press.

Harvey, E. L. (1994, March-April) Turning performance appraisals upside down. *Human Resources Professional*, *7* (2), 30-32.

Hazucha, J. F., Hezlett, S. A., & Schneider, R. J. (1993, Summer/Fall). The impact of 360-degree feedback on management skills development. *Human Resource Management*, *32* (2 & 3), 325-351.

Herman, S. M. (1972). Notes on freedom. In J.W. Pfeiffer & J.E. Jones (Eds.), *The 1972 annual handbook for group facilitators.* San Diego, CA: University Associates.

Hirsch, M. S. (1994, August). 360-degree evaluation. *Working Woman*, 20-21.

Hoffman, R. (1995, April). Ten reasons you should be using 360-degree feedback. *HR Magazine*, 82-85.

Johnson, E. K. (1990). *Total quality management and performance appraisal: To be or not to be? A literature review and case studies.* Unpublished draft, U.S. Office of Personnel Management, Research and Demonstration Division, Washington, DC.

Jones, J. E. (1980). Developing theoretical models. In J. E. Jones & J. W. Pfeiffer (Eds.), *The 1980 annual handbook for group facilitators.* San Diego, CA: University Associates.

Jones, J. E. (1990, December). Don't smile about smile sheets. *Training and Development Journal*, 19-21.

Jones, J. E., & Bearley, W. L. (1994a). *Management skills assessment system: User's guide.* Valley Center, CA: Organizational Universe Systems.

Jones, J. E., & Bearley, W. L. (1994b). *Teambook: 27 exercises for enhancing work groups.* King of Prussia, PA: Organization Design and Development.

Jones, J. E., & Bearley, W. L. (1995a). *Organizational change-readiness scale.* Amherst, MA: HRD Press.

Jones, J. E., & Bearley, W. L. (1995b). *Surveying employees: A practical guidebook.* Amherst, MA: HRD Press.

Jones, J. E., & Bearley, W. L. (1995c). *Team learning system.* Amherst, MA: HRD Press.

Jones, J. E., & Woodcock, M. (1985). *Manual of management development.* Aldershot, Nottinghamshire, England: Gower.

Kahneman, D., Slovic, P., & Tversky, A. (1982). *Judgment under uncertainty: Heuristics and biases.* New York: Cambridge University Press.

Kenny, D. A., Albright, L., Malloy, T. E., & Kashy, D. A. (1994). Consensus in interpersonal perception: Acquaintance and the big five. Psychological Bulletin, *116*, (2), 245-258.

Kirkpatrick, D. L. (1975). Techniques for evaluating training programs. In D. L. Kirkpatrick (Ed.), *Evaluating training programs.* Alexandria VA: American Society for Training and Development.

Kirkpatrick, D. L. (1983). *A practical guide for supervisory training and development.* Reading MA: Addison-Wesley.

Kirkpatrick, D. L. (1994). *Evaluating training programs: The four levels.* San Francisco, CA: Berrett-Kohler.

Korn/Ferry, Inc. (1989). *Reinventing the CEO.* New York, NY: Columbia Graduate School of Business.

Latham, G. P. (1989). Job performance and appraisal. In C. L. Cooper & J. Robertson (Eds.), *International review of industrial and organizational psychology.* New York: Wiley.

Lee, C. (1990, April). Talking back to the boss. *Training,* 29-34.

London, M., & Beatty, R. W. (1993). 360-degree feedback as a competitive advantage. *Human Resource Management, 32* (2 & 3), 353-372.

Miller, D. C. (1991). *Handbook of research design and social measurement.* Newbury Park, CA: Sage.

Mohrman, A. M. Jr., Resnick-West, S. M., & Lawler, E. E. III (1989). *Designing performance appraisal systems: Aligning appraisals and organizational realities.* San Francisco, CA: Jossey-Bass.

Morrison, A. M., McCall, M. W. Jr., & DeVries, D. L. (1978*). Feedback to managers: A comprehensive review of twenty-four instruments.* Greensboro, NC: Center for Creative Leadership.

Nilsen, D., & Campbell, D. P. (1993, Summer/Fall). Self-observer rating discrepancies: Once an overrater, always an overrater? *Human Resource Management, 32* (2 & 3), 265-281.

Nowack, K. M. (1993, January). 360-degree feedback: The whole story. *Training and Development, 47* (1), 69-72.

O'Reilly, B. (1994, October 17). Feedback can change your life. *Fortune,* 93-100.

Pareek, U., & Rao, T. V. (1974). *Handbook of psychological and social instruments.* Chamelbagh, Baroda, India: Samashti.

Peters, D. (1985). *Directory of human resource development instrumentation.* San Diego, CA: University Associates.

Pfeiffer, J. W., & Jones, J. E. (1972). Openness, collusion, and feedback. In J. W. Pfeiffer & J. E. Jones (Eds.), *The 1972 annual handbook for group facilitators.* San Diego, CA: University Associates.

Redman, T. (1992). Upward and onward: Can staff appraise their managers? *Personnel Review, 21,* (7), 32-46.

Romano, C. (1994, March). Conquering the fear of feedback. *Personnel, 71* (3), 9-10.

Sashkin, M. (1992, May 3). *Performance appraisal for total quality management.* Paper presented at the annual meeting of the Society for Industrial and Organizational Psychology, Montreal, Canada.

Schutz, W. (1994). *The human element: Productivity, self-esteem, and the bottom line.* San Francisco: Jossey-Bass.

Shaver, W. Jr. (1995). *How to build and use a 360-degree feedback system.* Alexandria, VA: American Society for Training and Development.

Shaw, M. E., & Wright, J. M. (1967). *Scales for the measurement of attitudes.* New York, NY: McGraw-Hill.

Smither, J. W., Wohlers, A. J., & London, M. (1995, March). A field study of reactions to normative versus individualized upward feedback. *Group and Organizational Management, 20* (1), 61-89.

Spector, P. E. (1981). *Research Designs.* Beverly Hills, CA: Sage.

Spencer, L. M., & Spencer, S. M. (1993.) *Competence at work: Models for superior performance.* New York: John Wiley & Sons.

Timmreck, C. W. (1995, May). *Upward feedback in the trenches: Challenges and realities.* Presentation at the Annual Conference of the Society for Industrial and Organizational Psychology, Orlando, FL.

Tornow, W. W. (1993, Summer-Fall). Perceptions or reality: Is multi-perspective measurement a means or an end? *Human Resources Management, 32* (2), 221-229.

Tornow, W. W. (1995). Upward feedback: The ups and downs of it. *Proposal to Society for Industrial and Organizational Psychology Symposium [for conducting a session].*

Velsor, E. V., & Leslie, J. B. (1991a). *Feedback to managers, 1991. Volume I: A guide to evaluating multi-rater feedback instruments.* Greensboro, NC: Center for Creative Leadership.

Velsor, E. V., & Leslie, J. B. (1991b). *Feedback to managers, 1991. Volume II: A review and comparison of sixteen multi-rater feedback instruments.* Greensboro, NC: Center for Creative Leadership.

Yukl, G. A. (1989). *Leadership in organizations.* Englewood Cliffs, NJ: Prentice-Hall.

Appendices

This section contains numerous resources for carrying out 360° feedback in organizations. Here is a brief description of its contents. Each of the appendices begins with a more detailed explanation of its content.

A. Logistical-Planning Worksheet. This form is useful for thinking through all of the steps that 360° feedback requires. The items may be adapted easily to a given application of this technology.

B. Sample 360° Feedback Action-Planning Worksheets. This appendix includes several worksheets that assist 360° feedback recipients in working through their data in order to develop plans for self-improvement. You can easily modify these forms to fit your feedback reports.

C. Survey of Needed Competencies. This anonymous survey is useful in establishing your client organizations' competency models. Use it in preparation for developing your 360° feedback questionnaire.

D. Data-Source Worksheet. This is a step-by-step approach to determining what data sources to include in 360° feedback, along with an optional system for establishing differential weights for these sources.

Appendix A

Logistical-Planning Worksheet for 360° Feedback

The following worksheet effectively guides the initial phase of planning the use of 360° feedback in organizations. Since the form is necessarily generic, you should adapt it to your particular application of this technology.

The importance of planning for 360° feedback cannot be overemphasized. For example, if there are ambiguities in the survey questionnaire, the data may be meaningless, and no amount of statistical manipulation can clean them up. If a reliable schedule of feedback sessions cannot be established, the feedback could be out of date before it is received.

The form includes those questions that we ask when we are consulting with clients who are considering using 360° feedback to help their people improve.

Logistical-Planning Worksheet

1. What is the *need* for 360° feedback?

2. What purpose(s) would 360° feedback serve in this planned application?

3. What leaders will receive individual, confidential feedback packages?

4. How many leaders will be involved?

5. What thematic content needs to be included in the survey questionnaire?

6. What existing sources could provide ideas for the content and format of the survey instrument?

7. Who will rate these leaders?

   - They will rate themselves.
   - Their supervisors will rate them.
   - They also will be rated by one or more other bosses, possibly including former ones.
   - Their colleagues or peers will rate them anonymously.
   - They will be rated by all of their subordinates anonymously.
   - They will be rated by their customers who are internal to the organization— non-anonymously.
   - They will solicit feedback from selected customers who are external to the organization.
   - They will be rated by members of their family and their friends.
   - They will be rated by others: _____

8. How will the ratings be collected?

   - Organizational mail
   - Mail to people's homes
   - Electronic mail
   - Mail/fax to a third-party processing center
   - Telephone response
   - Meetings for self-ratings, with leaders receiving questionnaires, which they then distribute
   - Other: _____

9. How will we ensure the security of the responses to the questionnaire, including how we protect anonymity and confidentiality?

10. What can we assume about the reading level and language proficiency of the raters?

11. How many people will probably respond to the survey, including all data sources?

12. Who needs to be involved in the development of this plan?

13. How will the confidential reports be fed back to the individual leaders?
    - Special meetings
    - Meetings by management level
    - As a component in a management-development course
    - In team-building sessions
    - One-on-one
    - Other: _____

14. What will be the form of the feedback reports?

15. Who will facilitate the feedback sessions?

16. What summary reports will go to the senior executive regarding trends in 360° feedback of organizational leaders? Who will prepare these reports and brief the top team?

17. How will the overall results be used in planning improvements in the organization's strategy for developing its leaders?

18. What could go wrong with this application, and how can that be prevented?

19. How will this application of 360° feedback be evaluated?

20. What is a realistic schedule for this project? Use the chart below to estimate time and establish starting and completion dates.

Schedule for 360° Feedback Tasks

Project Activity	Start	Complete
Approval of the 360° feedback project		
Establishment of needed competencies and skills		
Development of the survey instrument(s)		
Signoff on the survey instrument(s)		
Data collection		
Analysis and feedback-reports development		
Feedback to individual leaders		
Executive briefing design and reports development		
Executive briefing		
Evaluation of the project		

Appendix B

Sample 360° Feedback
Action-Planning Worksheets

The set of forms in this appendix make it easy for you to develop worksheets that precisely fit the formats of your statistical reports for individual 360° feedback recipients. The forms included are the following:

- **Isolating Strengths.** This form guides feedback recipients through an analysis of what strengths they can build on in making a self-directed plan for personal improvement.

- **Determining Areas of Improvement.** This form helps feedback participants to focus on a limited number of critical areas for planning improvements.

- **Force-Field Analysis.** This classic method makes it easy for feedback recipients to study each of their areas of needed improvement systematically.

- **Analyzing Support Resources.** Since 360° feedback recipients almost always need others' assistance in implementing their self-directed improvement plans, this form provides a method for inventorying these resources.

- **Criteria of Effective Plans: The SPIRO Model.** Use this page as the basis of a lecturette during feedback sessions, as a handout or as an enclosure in feedback packages.

- **Establishing Measures, Controls, and Rewards.** We have three truisms that guide most of our work within organizations:

    > What gets measured gets done.
    > What gets measured and fed back gets done well.
    > What gets rewarded gets repeated.

This form emphasizes all three of these principles.

- **Closing Perception Gaps.** This form, and the two pages that follow it, guide 360° feedback recipients through planning to discuss differences in how they see themselves and how others perceive them. They also help feedback recipients make plans to achieve closure on the entire 360° intervention.

- **Self-Directed Action Plan Timeline.** This form puts the entire plan on one page, with beginning and ending dates for each activity.

- **Commitment Statement.** We use this form to have 360° feedback recipients make oral statements to groups of peers in feedback sessions. We sometimes mail a copy back to feedback recipients a few weeks after the feedback session. Finally, we use the content of their statements to prepare follow-up survey questionnaires to be used to evaluate the 360° feedback intervention.

Isolating Strengths

Why This Is Important. In our culture it is often not OK for us to pay attention to our strengths. Your feedback package, however, contains a clear pattern of the ways in which you are perceived positively. The **Strength and Needs** report lists your "top" and "bottom" areas of competency.

The purposes of the task that you are about to undertake are the following:

- Taking personal credit
- Dealing from strength
- Overcoming the tendency to discount one's achievements
- Knowing what you're good at
- Capitalizing on your developed competencies

1. In the space below, copy the items that represent your outstanding strengths as identified by the **Strengths and Needs** report. Use a star to mark those of which you feel particularly proud.

2. Now write down any other significant strengths that you use in this organization.

3. Think back about your growth during your career. In the space below, specify how you developed the above strengths.

Determining Areas for Improvement

Why This Is Important. It has been said that more than three goals are no goals. The purpose of this task is to narrow your planning to those areas of competency that will be most beneficial for both you and your company. In creating your *Self-Directed Action Plan,* you will want to focus on only two or three areas.

1. In the space below, copy the items that represent your needs for improvement as identified by the **Strengths and Needs** report that you analyzed earlier.

2. Using the **Items by Average**, **Discrepancy,** and **Index Summary** reports, write down any other significant improvement needs that you have.

3. The Pareto Principle states that you can get 80% of your improvement from focusing on 20% of your improvement needs. Now go back to the lists that you write in Steps 1 and 2 above. Star those 2 or 3 areas for which you would get the greatest gain both for yourself and your company.

Force-Field Analysis

This worksheet helps you to think through each of the improvement areas that may become the basis of your *Self-Directed Action Plan*. Before deciding what actions you will take, analyze the situation thoroughly. Use a copy of this form for each of your selected areas.

1. Area of desired improvement:

2. What this is costing me right now:

3. Payoffs for improving myself in this area:

Forces Supporting and Resisting Your Improvement

Driving Forces	*Restraining Forces*
Behaviors, skills, and conditions that help me now or may have helped me in the past in this area	Behaviors, skills, or conditions that are holding me back right now or may have held me back in the past

My Status Quo Right Now

_____	_____
_____	_____
_____	_____
_____	_____
_____	_____
_____	_____
_____	_____

Analyzing Support Resources

This worksheet helps you to think through those sources of assistance you can bring to bear on your *Self-Directed Action Plan.*

1. **Your boss.** In the space below, write your thoughts about how your boss can assist you in your development.

2. **Your colleagues.** Write your thoughts about how your co-workers can support your *Self-Directed Action Plan.*

3. **Your family and friends.** How can you use your personal network to help you improve?

4. **Your company.** Think about company training, career-development programs, job rotation, task forces, special assignments, and so forth. What appeals to you right now?

5. **External resources.** Consider training, additional higher education, counseling, reading, audio- and videotapes, computer-assisted learning, and the like. What appeals to you right now?

Criteria of Effective Plans: The SPIRO Model

Use the following five criteria when developing your *Self-Directed Action Plan*. The goal here is to make a complete plan to which you are clearly committed. Think about being thorough and imaginative in creating the steps that you will take to benefit yourself, and your company.

S	**Specificity**	*What **exactly** are you going to do?*
P	**Performance**	*What do you intend to **accomplish**?*
I	**Involvement**	*What is **your** part in the plan?*
R	**Realism**	*Can it be done, given the resources available?*
O	**Observability**	*How will you know whether or not you have been successful?*

The acronym SPIRO, in Latin, literally means "I breathe." It is the root of words like "inspire" and "spirit." As you think through what you will commit to in terms of your personal and professional development, remember that these five criteria can help you maintain the discipline necessary to implement your plan successfully.

The SPIRO model is abstracted from *Criteria of effective goal setting: The SPIRO model,* by J. E. Jones. In J. W. Pfeiffer & J. E. Jones (Eds.), *The 1972 Annual Handbook for Group Facilitators.* San Diego: Pfeiffer and Company, 1972.

Establishing Measures, Controls, and Rewards

You have not completed your *Self-Directed Action Plan* until you have committed yourself to establishing systems for tracking your progress. The purpose of this form is to assist you in thinking through how you will find out how well you are doing in improving yourself, how you will prevent yourself from "backsliding," and how you will reward yourself when you become aware that you are indeed becoming an increasingly effective contributor to the success of your company.

1. What would be valid criteria for success in each of the areas of improvement that you have decided to focus on?

2. How can you get reliable information on how well you are doing with regard to each of these criteria?

3. In what ways can you sabotage your *Self-Directed Action Plan*?

4. How can you ensure that you will follow through on your commitment for improvement?

5. How can you reward yourself when you know that you are getting better in your chosen improvement areas—whether others notice or not?

Closing Perception Gaps

The report entitled **Largest Gaps between Self and Other Ratings** identifies those survey items on which you rated yourself differently than others rated you. The purpose of this worksheet is to help you think through whether you need to do anything about these gaps in perceptions and to consider making closing these gaps a part of your improvement plan.

1. Look at the **Gap** report and ask yourself, "Are the differences big enough to be significant to me?"

2. Where were the greatest differences? (Identify which individual or group responses were most different from your own.)

3. On what skills were there the greatest perception gaps? Star those areas that you have already decided to improve.

4. Whom do you need to talk with about these gaps?

5. Commit yourself to soliciting additional feedback and/or clarification as part of your *Self-Directed Action Plan.*

Planning a Meeting with Your Boss

In following through with the people who gave you feedback, you should seriously consider having a meeting with your manager. You will undoubtedly need his or her assistance in carrying out your *Self-Directed Action Plan*. This form helps you develop a plan for meeting with your boss about your *Self-Directed Action Plan*.

Here is an outline of such a meeting:

Prework: Set a realistic career target for yourself, a position you would hope to be in three to five years from now. Then write your manager a positive note about your wish to confer on your *Self-Directed Action Plan*. Set a definite time for the meeting, which should run for about an hour.

The Meeting: Thank your manager for taking the time to meet with you. Specify the objectives of this meeting:

- To understand your *Self-Directed Action Plan*.

- To resolve any gaps between how you perceive your skills and how your manager sees your skills.

- To enroll your manager in supporting your skills development and career goals within the company.

Follow these steps during the meeting:

1. Summarize your feedback, pointing out both your strengths and areas for improvement. Draw attention to differences between your self-ratings and those of your manager. Talk these through.

2. Tell your manager what you intend to do to improve your critical skills and what your career goal is, and enroll him or her in supporting you.

3. Set a definite date for checking up on your progress in implementing your *Self-Directed Action Plan*.

4. Things to **avoid** in this meeting: defensiveness, putting your manager on the spot, denying what the data say about you, discounting the validity of others' ratings, and fuzzy, nonspecific plans.

Meeting with Other Feedback Providers

In following through with the people who gave you feedback, you should seriously consider having a meeting with them. You will undoubtedly need their assistance in carrying out your *Self-Directed Action Plan*. This form helps you develop a plan for meeting with your people about your plan. This meeting could be in a group or one-on-one. Here is an outline of such a meeting:

Prework: Write to all of the people who rated you (actually, to all of the *groups* of people, since some of your ratings may have been anonymous). This should be a positive memorandum about your wish to confer on your *Self-Directed Action Plan*. Set a definite time for the meeting, which should run for about an hour.

The Meeting: Thank your people for rating you and for taking the time to meet with you. Specify the objectives of this meeting:

- To understand your *Self-Directed Action Plan*.

- To resolve any gaps between how you perceive your skills and how they see your skills.

- To enroll them in supporting your skills development and career development.

Follow these steps during the meeting:

1. Summarize your feedback, pointing out both your strengths and weaknesses. Draw attention to differences between your self-ratings and theirs. Talk these through.

2. Tell them what you intend to do to improve your critical skills, and enroll them in supporting you.

3. Set a definite date for checking up on your progress in implementing your *Self-Directed Action Plan*.

4. Things to **avoid** in this meeting: defensiveness, putting people on the spot, denying what the data say about you, discounting the validity of their ratings, and fuzzy, nonspecific plans.

Self-Directed Action Plan Timeline

This worksheet helps you develop a Gantt chart of the activities and tasks that will lead to your improvement as a manager. Across the top, write abbreviations for the next 12 months (Jan., Feb., and so forth). In the left-hand column, write the sequence of actions that you plan to take. Beside each step, write X's for the start and completion times for each activity, and connect the pairs of X's with straight lines, to form horizontal bars. These lines may overlap each other; that is, one activity can begin before another has been finished.

		One Year
Action-Plan Step	**Today** . / . / . / . / . / . / . / . / . / . / . / . / .	**From Now**
_____	. / . / . / . / . / . / . / . / . / . / . / . / .	
_____	. / . / . / . / . / . / . / . / . / . / . / . / .	
_____	. / . / . / . / . / . / . / . / . / . / . / . / .	
_____	. / . / . / . / . / . / . / . / . / . / . / . / .	
_____	. / . / . / . / . / . / . / . / . / . / . / . / .	
_____	. / . / . / . / . / . / . / . / . / . / . / . / .	
_____	. / . / . / . / . / . / . / . / . / . / . / . / .	
_____	. / . / . / . / . / . / . / . / . / . / . / . / .	
_____	. / . / . / . / . / . / . / . / . / . / . / . / .	
_____	. / . / . / . / . / . / . / . / . / . / . / . / .	
_____	. / . / . / . / . / . / . / . / . / . / . / . / .	
_____	. / . / . / . / . / . / . / . / . / . / . / . / .	
_____	. / . / . / . / . / . / . / . / . / . / . / . / .	
_____	. / . / . / . / . / . / . / . / . / . / . / . / .	
_____	. / . / . / . / . / . / . / . / . / . / . / . / .	

Commitment Statement

In the space below, complete the sentence in your own words. Then give this form to someone you trust, and ask that person to mail it back to you after about a month. Make a second copy for yourself. The purpose is to reinforce your commitment to take personal responsibility for implementing your *Self-Directed Action Plan.*

As a result of my feedback, I intend to . . .

Your Signature: _____

Your Mailing Address: _____

_____

_____

Today's Date: _____

Appendix C

Survey of Needed Competencies

This appendix contains a special questionnaire that is useful for developing competency models. Use it to conduct an anonymous survey of top leadership (or managers in general); then work with the senior executives to specify the competencies their people need in order to realize the vision of the organization.

We developed this survey questionnaire from a comprehensive study of models of leadership and management. We typically use the *Survey of Needed Competencies* to survey a random sample of managers; then we survey the senior-executive cadre. In a work session with the top team, we publish the comparative statistics and facilitate the choosing of competencies to include in the target 360° assessment instrument. The discussion includes "wordsmithing" the items. This process assures both maximum content validity for the instrument and commitment on the part of senior leaders to support the 360° feedback intervention.

Survey of Needed Competencies

Instructions: This is an anonymous survey, and the results will be presented to the executive team and summarized for the senior-executive group. Using the scale below, indicate how important each of the following competencies is for people who lead others within the organization. Record your rating in the space next to each competency.

10	Very highly important	5	Somewhat unimportant
9		4	
8	Highly important	3	Unimportant
7		2	
6	Somewhat important	1	Definitely unimportant

_____   1. Motivating others effectively.

_____   2. Explaining new tasks clearly.

_____   3. Handling stress well.

_____   4. Giving others constructive criticism.

_____   5. Overseeing projects effectively.

_____   6. Managing conflict skillfully.

_____   7. Showing consideration for others.

_____   8. Working well with others in setting goals.

_____   9. Maintaining discipline effectively.

_____   10. Establishing clear expectations.

_____   11. Representing the work group effectively to the next level up.

_____   12. Managing change effectively.

_____   13. Giving others recognition for their accomplishments.

_____   14. Letting others know how well they are doing.

_____   15. Dealing effectively with ambiguity.

Please continue on the next page.

10	Very highly important	5	Somewhat unimportant
9		4	
8	Highly important	3	Unimportant
7		2	
6	Somewhat important	1	Definitely unimportant

_____ 16. Behaving ethically.

_____ 17. Helping others to see the importance of their work.

_____ 18. Working well with people from different cultures.

_____ 19. Delegating tasks appropriately.

_____ 20. Inspiring others.

_____ 21. Orienting new employees well.

_____ 22. Providing emotional support.

_____ 23. Confronting others in a skillful manner.

_____ 24. Promoting effective teamwork.

_____ 25. Negotiating effectively.

_____ 26. Working comfortably whether alone or with others.

_____ 27. Showing effective planning skills.

_____ 28. Involving people in decisions that affect them.

_____ 29. Treating others fairly.

_____ 30. Conducting appraisal interviews effectively.

_____ 31. Cooperating well with others.

_____ 32. Working well with people of the opposite sex.

_____ 33. Managing relations with other departments well.

_____ 34. Helping people develop their abilities.

_____ 35. Being receptive to feedback.

Please continue on the next page.

10	Very highly important	5	Somewhat unimportant
9		4	
8	Highly important	3	Unimportant
7		2	
6	Somewhat important	1	Definitely unimportant

_____ 36. Persuading others skillfully.

_____ 37. Getting things organized.

_____ 38. Participating actively in organizational activities.

_____ 39. Giving opinions freely when appropriate.

_____ 40. Thinking futuristically.

_____ 41. Making necessary decisions right away.

_____ 42. Showing commitment to the priorities of the organization.

_____ 43. Doing trouble-shooting effectively.

_____ 44. Managing time effectively.

_____ 45. Running good meetings.

_____ 46. Adapting supervision to individuals.

_____ 47. Representing the organization outside effectively.

_____ 48. Looking for new ways to develop business for the organization.

_____ 49. Playing organizational politics well.

_____ 50. Taking reasonable risks.

_____ 51. Coaching others in developing skills.

_____ 52. Solving problems skillfully.

_____ 53. Working well with others.

_____ 54. Showing sensitivity to others' feelings.

_____ 55. Creating useful ideas and procedures.

Please continue on the next page.

10	Very highly important	5	Somewhat unimportant
9		4	
8	Highly important	3	Unimportant
7		2	
6	Somewhat important	1	Definitely unimportant

_____   56. Expressing feelings openly.

_____   57. Listening to and communicating well with individuals.

_____   58. Actively participating in community activities.

_____   59. Making things happen.

_____   60. Demonstrating a good sense of humor.

_____   61. Showing loyalty to the organization.

_____   62. Fitting into the organization well.

_____   63. Controlling costs effectively.

_____   64. Facilitating group consensus.

_____   65. Engaging in succession planning effectively.

_____   66. Hiring people effectively.

_____   67. Coordinating others' work activities well.

_____   68. Making effective oral presentations.

_____   69. Scheduling work tasks effectively.

_____   70. Pushing for "bottom-line" results.

_____   71. Using subordinate suggestions well.

_____   72. Staying up-to-date in his or her professional field.

_____   73. Accepting constraints effectively.

_____   74. Performing staff reductions effectively.

_____   75. Counseling with direct reports on personal concerns.

Please continue on the next page.

10	Very highly important	5	Somewhat unimportant
9		4	
8	Highly important	3	Unimportant
7		2	
6	Somewhat important	1	Definitely unimportant

_____ 76. Providing appropriate resources for subordinates.

_____ 77. Monitoring the task performance of subordinates.

_____ 78. Dismissing employees in a sensitive manner.

_____ 79. Making command decisions when appropriate.

_____ 80. Maintaining performance standards.

_____ 81. Giving direct reports the authority to do their work.

_____ 82. Following through on required paperwork.

_____ 83. Keeping job roles clear.

_____ 84. Meeting deadlines.

_____ 85. Showing a high level of productivity these days.

_____ 86. Showing promise for significant advancement in the organization.

_____ 87. Other _____

_____ 88. Other _____

Thank you for your cooperation in this important study. Return this form right away in the envelope provided.

Appendix D

Data-Source Worksheet

This appendix contains a form to use with the people who approve your 360° feedback interventions. It facilitates their specifying who will be the raters in the intervention and, optionally, how much weight each of these data sources will receive in statistical reports. The *Data-Source Worksheet* makes it easy for you to facilitate a discussion of the credibility of various sources of 360° assessment ratings. The people who approve your interventions may, of course, choose not to establish differential weights for the data sources.

Adapt the worksheet to fit your needs in obtaining the guidance and "buy-in" you need from the senior leadership team.

Data-Source Worksheet

The Management Skills Assessment System involves collecting ratings on managers from four sources: the managers themselves, the persons to whom they report, their peers, and their subordinates.

Task 1. Selecting raters. In the 360° feedback intervention, we will be collecting data from multiple raters. Using the checklist below, discuss and specify as a group who will rate the feedback recipients.

- The feedback recipients themselves—self-ratings.
- The persons to whom these people report—boss ratings.
- The persons with whom these individuals work—peer/colleague ratings.
- The persons who report directly to the feedback recipients—subordinate ratings.
- Customers of these individuals, internal to the organization—internal-customer ratings.
- Customers of these individuals who are external to the organization—external-customer ratings.
- Friends and families of these individuals—friends/family ratings.
- Other _____
- Other _____

Task 2. Rank-ordering the data sources. The purpose of this task is to solicit your independent judgment on the weight or importance that your group attaches to each of the four data sources. In the space in front of each data source below, indicate your sense of the data source's relative rank. Place the number 1 in front of the most important source, the number 2 in front of the second most important source, the number 3 in front of the third most important source, and the number 4 in front of the comparatively least important source.

Rank	Data Source
_____	Self
_____	Boss
_____	Peers/colleagues
_____	Subordinates
_____	Internal-customers
_____	External-customers
_____	Friends/family
_____	_____
_____	_____

Task 3. Developing group consensus on the ranks of the data sources. Using the following chart, share your rankings with the other members of your group. After filling in the rankings of all the members, add up the ratings across each row and write the sums in the sum column. Finally, using the sums, place the rank of each item in the rank column. Rank the item with the lowest sum 1, rank the item with the next lowest sum 2, and so forth. (If there are more than five members of your group, do this task on a flipchart or overhead transparency.)

	Your Rank	OTHER GROUP MEMBERS A	B	C	D	Sum	Group Rank
Self	_____	_____	_____	_____	_____	_____	_____
Boss	_____	_____	_____	_____	_____	_____	_____
Peers	_____	_____	_____	_____	_____	_____	_____
Subordinates	_____	_____	_____	_____	_____	_____	_____
Internals	_____	_____	_____	_____	_____	_____	_____
Externals	_____	_____	_____	_____	_____	_____	_____
Friends/Fam.	_____	_____	_____	_____	_____	_____	_____
_____	_____	_____	_____	_____	_____	_____	_____
_____	_____	_____	_____	_____	_____	_____	_____

Task 4. Rating the credibility of the data sources. In the space in front of each data source below, copy the group rank from the table above. In the space to the right of each data source, write your judgment of the appropriate weight for each data source. Begin by writing a 10 to the right of the source ranked 1 by the group. To the right of the remaining data sources, write a number from 0 to 10 to show your perception of its relative weight in comparison with the first item and to the other items. If you think all four are equally important, write a 10 by all sources. If you think a data source is invalid or irrelevant, write a 0 to the right of that item. Remember, your points represent your judgment about how credible these sources of ratings are for this 360° feedback intervention. They will be combined with the other group members' to generate consensus on the weights that the data sources will receive in the statistical analyses of the ratings data.

_____	Self		_____	Internal-customers
_____	Boss		_____	External-customers
_____	Peers/colleagues		_____	Friends/family
_____	Subordinates		_____	_____
_____	_____		_____	_____

Task 5. Establishing weights for the data sources. In the table below, copy your ratings and those of the other members of your group. Then discuss these to arrive at a common set of weights for the data sources. The final weights should be between 0 (no weight) and 1 (maximum weight). Express the weights as decimals.

	Your Rank	OTHER GROUP MEMBERS				Sum	Group Weight
		A	B	C	D		
Self	_____	_____	_____	_____	_____	_____	_____
Boss	_____	_____	_____	_____	_____	_____	_____
Peers	_____	_____	_____	_____	_____	_____	_____
Subordinates	_____	_____	_____	_____	_____	_____	_____
Internals	_____	_____	_____	_____	_____	_____	_____
Externals	_____	_____	_____	_____	_____	_____	_____
Friends/Fam.	_____	_____	_____	_____	_____	_____	_____
_____	_____	_____	_____	_____	_____	_____	_____
_____	_____	_____	_____	_____	_____	_____	_____

Index

Other Resources from Jones & Bearley and HRD Press

Surveying Employees: A Practical Guidebook

A "how-to" handbook for anyone who plans, administers, analyzes data from, or feeds back the results of organizational surveys. This book spells out, in step-by-step methods, all of the critical considerations regarding employee-opinion, climate, "culture," quality, and customer surveys. Chapters cover such topics as logistical planning, using a task force, developing questionnaires, preparing reports, feeding back results one-on-one and to work groups, reliability and validity, and norms. Jones & Bearley have consulted with numerous organizations, in both the public and private sectors, on all kinds of employee surveys, and their considerable experience makes this book both practical and theoretically sound.

Team Learning System

This unique Windows™ software makes it easy for teams to "take their own pulse." The system includes two questionnaires, *Right Things Right* and *Team Player Assessment*. The first facilitates identifying team time-wasters, and the second facilitates a complete exchange of feedback among team members, a sort of "90° feedback" experience. The printed forms are customized to include the team's name and the names of the individual team members. The system can be used with or without a facilitator.

Tips, Tricks, Tools, & Techniques for Trainers

Developed in collaboration with Doug Watsabaugh, this book includes hundreds of down-to-earth "dos and don'ts" for trainers, facilitators, and consultants. Included are training exercises, instruments, models, training designs, and practical information that can optimize the training that you may already be carrying out. The book includes all of the handouts, instruments, overhead transparencies, and worksheets on diskette, so that you can easily customize them for use in your sessions. In addition, there are PowerPoint™ presentations that you can use in your training sessions to make your lecturettes come alive with color and movement.

Organizational Change-Readiness Scale

An instrument you can use in training sessions, team building, and organizational consulting. The scale helps participants analyze the supports for, and barriers to, change within their organization. An action-planning system is built into the instrument booklet. The instrument is useful in working with key leaders one-on-one, in management-development courses, in executive offsites, and in coaching supervisors.

Managing Your Energy

An assessment of burnout symptoms and how to avoid having them dissipate your energy. This instrument booklet contains not only the questionnaire but also the theory base, practical methods for maintaining your personal energy, norms for about 1000 people nationwide, and complete action-planning worksheets. This instrument could complement 360° feedback, especially for persons who may be "under norm" in their multi-rater results.

The Authors

John E. Jones. President of Organizational Universe Systems (OUS), John probably is best known as co-editor of experience-based training and consulting handbooks and annuals. As an experienced trainer, presenter, counselor, professor, entrepreneur, and consultant, he effectively bridges the theoretical and the practical. He consults widely, with such clients as Air Canada, ARC International (U.S.A. & Japan), AT&T Bell Laboratories, AT&T Consumer Products, Canadian Air Force, Coca-Cola, Coors Brewing Company, Fletcher Challenge Canada, General Motors, Holiday Inns, Kaiser-Permanente, McKesson, Network Management, Owens-Corning, Psychological Associates, Public Service Electric & Gas, Rockwell Telecommunications, SAP Americas, Shearson-Lehman Mortgage, The Prudential, Tonka, Turner Construction, Unisys, Wallace Computer Services, Xerox, and numerous not-for-profit organizations in education, government, and health care. Dr. Jones taught at the University of Iowa for eight years, in the field of counselor education. He has lectured widely on a wide range of topics in education, training, organization behavior, and leadership. His special interests in development are training design and delivery, executive team building, intergroup problem solving, organizational survey feedback, and management development. He has collaborated with Dr. William L. Bearley on state-of-the-art survey software and management-training instruments.

William L. Bearley. Vice President of Organizational Universe Systems, Bill has a variety of experiences as a teacher, professor, trainer, consultant, and businessperson. He is unique in that he is thoroughly educated in both computer science and behavioral science. Thus, he brings considerable breadth of perspective to the practice of developing and improving management systems. He has pioneered the fusion of organization development with the introduction of management information systems in organizations. Bill consults with numerous clients, such as AT&T Communications, AT&T Bell Laboratories, Honeywell, Xerox, Loreal, McKesson, Kaiser-Permanente, Equifax, and many educational and health-care organizations. Dr. Bearley is a graduate of the University Associates intern program and currently serves as a professor in the doctoral program in educational management at the University of La Verne.

Organizational Universe Systems

Specializing in management/leadership development and organization development, OUS is a pioneer in the development of employee-survey and 360° feedback software. Numerous organizations use the **Organizational Universe Survey System** and the **Management Skills Assessment System** to create, process, and report on a wide array of surveys. OUS can be contacted at P.O. Box 38, Valley Center, CA 92082. Telephone 619/749-0811; FAX 619/749-8051; E-mail jejones@ix.netcom.com or wlbearley@ix.netcom.com.

Performance Skills Leader

PS Leader is a research-based leadership competency assessment that gives leaders an objective needs analysis of their leadership effectiveness, and helps them target areas for improvement. The core of the assessment is a set of 24 clearly defined competencies that have been shown to be an essential part of effective leader performance.

PS Leader is:

- **Cost Effective**—Only $65.00 per leader!

- **Flexible**—This multi-rater assessment can be used as a leader self-assessment or with supervisors, peers, and subordinates for 360 degree feedback.

- **Easy to administer**—*PS Leader* is computerized, so participants simply follow on-screen instructions for completing the 82-item questionnaire and saving their answers.

- **Confidential**—Once respondents have saved their answers, they are locked on the diskette. This guarantee of confidentiality will allow peers and subordinates to feel comfortable giving honest feedback.

- **Relevant feedback**—Rather than answering questions about particular leadership competencies that can be difficult or impossible to make judgements on, respondents are asked about specific behaviors associated with these competencies. By rating these *observable* behaviors, the assessment provides a method for accurately measuring competencies.

- **Convenient** —Once the questionnaire has been completed, the diskette is returned to HRD Press for scoring and report generation. You just decide which reports you want and mail in the diskette, and you will receive the results in about one week!

- **Group reports are available**—Now your HR department can plan for development needs corporate-wide!

Also Available:
PS Supervisor
PS Team Leader
PS Teams

Call HRD Press to review an example set of Individual Feedback Reports.

HRD Press • 22 Amherst Road • Amherst, MA 01002
1-800-860-1361 • FAX 413-253-2390